Jordan L. Harding

COLLECTION

Class of
1950

Doctor of Laws (Honorary)
2002

SHENANDOAH
UNIVERSITY

BALZAC & THE NOVEL

BALZAC

& THE NOVEL

by *Samuel Rogers*

Madison • The UNIVERSITY of
WISCONSIN PRESS • 1953

Printed in the United States of America by
The William Byrd Press, Incorporated
Richmond, Virginia

To

George Clarke Sellery

with gratitude and affection

Preface

Thousands of books and articles have been written about Balzac. Surely no other novelist has received more careful study, and yet in the hundred years since his death no general agreement has been reached as to either the nature or the value of *La Comédie humaine.* Balzac has been called the novelist most different from Dostoievksi; he has also been hailed as one of Dostoievski's prophets. It has been said that he derived all his subjects from intimate personal experience; it has also been said that he never chose them for special or private reasons. Psychologically, he has been classed as a *visuel,* an *auditif,* or, in distinction to either of these, a *sentimental.* Both royalists and Marxists have acclaimed his description of society. To some critics he is an energetic dauber; to others he is one of the great novelists of the world.

To live intimately with Balzac is dangerous: one may fall under his spell, and then it is hard to resist writing about him. No matter how much one admires the brilliance, the wisdom, and the scope of Balzac criticism, one begins to feel that there is something, and always will be something, that remains to be said. His world, in its vastness and unity, is like a solar system: we may discover, or think we have discovered, the laws that control it; we may have theories about its evolution; but we should not be too surprised if at any time some fresh insight gave each detail, each law a slightly different meaning, pushing back the mystery one step further yet never fully revealing it.

The present study is addressed first of all to the American reader interested in the serious novel. One should not pass judgment upon any writer without having read his complete works; but it seems to me that one may form a fair idea of the genius of Dostoievski or Tolstoi, of Dickens or Jane Austen, of Stendhal or Flaubert from a few of their greatest books. Such is not the case with Balzac. *La Comédie humaine,* vast as it is, uncompleted as it was bound to be, is none the less a unit. As you begin each story or novel, your enjoyment and your understanding are increased by the sense of all the others clustered about it. There is, woven into the tissue of *La Comédie humaine* with its warp and woof of space and time, a multitude of cross-allusions, direct and implied, which, like those in *Ulysses,* cannot be grasped in a fragmentary reading; yet few Americans have the time or the patience to explore it as a whole. Quite apart from its enormous length, it probably offers at first, even to the most willing reader, more discouraging barriers than the work of any other major novelist.

My aim is to present a broad picture of *La Comédie humaine* that may serve as a context into which the reader can fit the particular novels and stories he happens to know. It is interesting to follow the ripening of Balzac's art from his youthful adventure stories, published under various pseudonyms, to *Eugénie Grandet* and *Le Père Goriot;* but the period between the earliest tales included in the *Comédie* and the mature novels is so short, and Balzac is so apt in later works to revert to the tricks of his youth that it seemed more helpful to present *La Comédie humaine* as it stands before posterity, in its almost incredible mass and volume, than to try to analyze the steps by which it came into being. In his own arrangement and frequent re-arrangements of the various parts, Balzac did not consider the order in which they were written, or even the order of the events they narrate. My picture of the *Comédie,* then, might be described as a panorama rather than a progress.

Balzac lived through and described an exceptionally crowded and interesting period. The air was full of social and political, religious and aesthetic ideas and systems, merging into each other or struggling against each other. There is hardly one of these that is not reflected in *La Comédie humaine.* Friedrich Engels has written: "I have learned more [from Balzac] than from all the professional historians, economists and statisticians put together."[1] One can start from *La Comédie humaine* as a center and proceed indefinitely in any direction.

This book is not primarily concerned with biographical detail or with Balzac's beliefs and the manner in which they reflect their time. None the less, since Balzac —like any other artist—had to create his works from his own experience, whether in the realm of personal relationships or that of ideas, such topics cannot be entirely passed over. Before approaching *La Comédie humaine* itself, I shall describe some of the raw materials out of which he was to construct this fictional universe: that is to say, his historical and social background and his attitudes toward it, the books he read,

[1] From a letter to Margaret Harkness written by Engels in 1888. Karl Marx and Frederick Engels, *Literature and Art: Selections from Their Writings* (New York, 1947), p. 43.

the people he knew. This first part, however, is introductory. Long and scholarly studies have been written
about aspects of his life or thought that I discuss in a
few paragraphs. The substance of what I have to say is
contained in the last three parts.

Throughout the book there are many excerpts from
Balzac's works and from his correspondence. All of
these I have translated. Sentences or phrases have sometimes been omitted, but I have not broken up my translations by the usual rows of dots. Footnotes refer the
reader to the original texts of all passages of more than
one or two lines. The edition of Balzac used, except for
the youthful works and a few early prefaces, is the
Oeuvres complètes de Honoré de Balzac in forty volumes published by Conard. In references to this edition,
the title of the individual work is listed first, then the
number of the volume in roman numerals, and then
the page.

I should like here to express my gratitude to my
friend and colleague William T. Bandy, who carefully
read through two different versions of my typescript
and made many wise suggestions. I want also to thank
Julian Harris, Max Otto, Gertrude Slaughter, and
Casimir Zdanowicz for their continued interest and
encouragement during the years that I was working
on this study.

CONTENTS

CONTENTS

PART I

The Materials

Whoever would raise himself above men must be prepared for a struggle.

—*Illusions perdues*

1

As we read the novels of Stendhal and Flaubert, we presently catch the hint, beneath the irony or the apparent objectivity, of a secret refuge which each man has constructed in the depths of his own mind, a refuge to which none but "the happy few" may be admitted and which makes life outside bleak and bitter by contrast. Once the signal has come through, the whole work is illumined from within, and we feel a personal friendship for the writer. "If I had known him," we think, "I could have given him the understanding he sought and so rarely found." We cannot be familiar with Balzac in quite this way: he is too massive, too turbulent, too various. If Stendhal wrote his novels in an attempt—at once desperate and lucid—to explain to himself the mystery of his own nature, if Flaubert wrote his in an equally desperate struggle to escape from himself into the realm of Absolute Beauty, Balzac was so obsessed by his imaginary world that, when confronted with his subject, he forgot himself entirely. He is not so much hidden, mysteriously intact, deep in the center of his work, like Stendhal or Flaubert, as diffused all through it, identified equally with every part and yet distinct from every part. He is himself both the one and the many.

Champfleury, half-forgotten novelist of the generation following Balzac's, accurately refers to him as "the great artist at once so personal and so impersonal." Balzac was fascinated by everything with which he

3

came into contact: spiritualism, science, philosophy, music, politics, great books and cheap novels, the streets of Paris, the closed blinds and peering eyes of the provinces. There is not one of his personal interests and enthusiasms, not one of his most secret fears and urges that has not left its mark on *La Comédie humaine.* "Believe me, Monsieur," says Benassis, the country doctor, "those who have probed most deeply into the vices and virtues of human nature are people who have studied it sincerely in themselves. We proceed from ourselves to men, never from men to ourselves."[1] Anyone familiar with Balzac's career and temperament must realize how these words apply to the good doctor's creator.

One might set against them, however, a statement of Gertrude Stein's: "I am not I any longer when I see." Balzac might have made the same remark. He starts with himself, yes, but he does proceed to men; and when he has taken that step, the distinction between himself and the rest of the world disappears. Let me give one trifling example. As a young man, Balzac assumed the ennobling particle *de* to which he had no right, or (to do him justice) resumed the use of it which his father had originated. If it is possible that at first because of his father's example he believed it was authentic, he must soon have been enlightened. Contemporary critics and journalists loved to make fun of it; even the great Sainte-Beuve alludes to it. One would fancy, therefore, that such a procedure would be the last thing

[1] *Le Médecin de campagne* in *Oeuvres complètes de Honoré de Balzac* (ed. Bouteron and Longnon, Paris: Louis Conard, 1912–40), XXIV, 204. Roman numerals in the following footnote references to Balzac's works indicate the volume number of the *Oeuvres complètes.*

4

Balzac would wish to refer to in his own work; and yet from the early *Annette et le criminel* (1824)— written before he made the change—where Monsieur Lesecq suddenly becoming rich reappears as Monsieur de Secq, to the play *La Marâtre* (1848) where the bourgeois Monsieur Godard insists on being called Godard de Rimonville, at least ten of his characters assume the unwarranted *de* for much the same reason that Balzac himself did.[2]

This example, I realize, is trivial. I have used it because it is so specific, and because it illustrates in a sharp, small way a general tendency. It may help to show why, each from his own point of view, the critics are right when they describe Balzac as either personal or objective. He had to the highest degree the faculty of identifying himself with the lives of others and watching his own life, his own attitudes as if they were those of someone else. Ultimately he saw everything, whether within himself or in the society about him, as material—material which, by a vigorous act of creation, he was to arrange, to combine, to transform into *La Comédie humaine.*

2

Born on the twentieth of May, 1799, during the last months of the Directorate and living through the Consulate, the Empire, the Restoration, and the July Monarchy, Balzac faced a restless and changing world. If

[2] There are also several places where one character uses the *de* in addressing another, like La Fontaine's fox, as a means of crude flattery.

the revolution of 1848 came too late to be reflected in his work, the great Revolution was still near enough to have a sense of actuality, and he grew up among people who had lived part of their lives under the Monarchy. His father, born in 1746, was in many ways a type of the eighteenth-century *philosophe* and social reformer, a man of exceptional energy and a variety of interests who, by his optimistic shrewdness throughout a long career, lifted himself from his peasant background into the ranks of the well-to-do bourgeoisie. Even Madame de Berny, the first woman Balzac loved, and the woman he loved best, had childhood memories of the *ancien régime*. She was twelve years old at the outbreak of the Revolution; her father had been a musician at the court of Louis XVI, and she herself was a goddaughter of Marie Antoinette. Honoré was old enough to remember the excitement of the last days of the Empire, the spell cast by Napoleon, whose shadow stretches across *La Comédie humaine;* and it was in contrast to these earlier periods that, like many of his contemporaries, he saw the Restoration and the July Monarchy.

The Napoleonic years, with their mixture of glory, hardship, and melodrama, lived again in the memory of the people; the Emperor's very weaknesses combined with his genius to make him appear, after his spectacular fall, as a hero at once mythical and human. Croce speaks of "the marvelous idealizing transformation, the admiration, the fanaticism, the regret, the tenderness, that was to be observed in all countries for Napoleon,"[3] and this was nowhere more evident than in

[3] Benedetto Croce, *History of Europe in the Nineteenth Century* (London, 1939), p. 83.

France. The multiplying echo of his greatness helps give historical perspective not only to *La Comédie humaine* but also to the novels of Stendhal and to many of the works of Victor Hugo.

The shrewdness of Louis XVIII, the futile charm of Charles X, on the other hand, offered their subjects small chance for poetic idealization. The French people, exhausted by twenty-five years of revolution and of dictatorships, accepted the return of the Bourbons without enthusiasm. Even those classes most eager for the Restoration, the nobles, the priests, the upper bourgeoisie, seem to have welcomed it chiefly as a means for revenge, for recapturing power, for making money. The July Monarchy under the "bourgeois king" Louis Philippe is certainly no more inspiring. If the years between 1815 and 1848 with their leftist uprisings, their rightist conspiracies, their threats of war seemed more eventful to those who lived through them than they seem to us today, they lack the world-drama that had filled—in wave after wave, at once exhilarating and terrifying—the quarter of a century from the fall of the Bastille to the battle of Waterloo. In the light of the great Revolution, the overthrow of Charles X appears trivial indeed; the crazy attempt of the Duchesse de Berry to win the throne for her son is romantic farce compared with the tragedy of Marie Antoinette; and even the gallant death of "the four sergeants of La Rochelle" in 1822 for refusing to betray their fellow-conspirators dwindles to a minor episode if seen against the background of Moscow and Austerlitz.

When we turn, however, from national events to examine the structure of Restoration society, we see that the period was filled with a special drama of its own, a drama of perpetually shifting contrasts, of innumerable private struggles, of incongruous juxtapositions. There was still desperate poverty; there was great and newly acquired wealth. While some men were clutching at the past, seeing it nostalgically across the gulf of the Revolution as a kind of lost paradise, others were struggling to build a future that would escape forever from that very past. Saint-Simon was preaching that the whole of human society should be administered by an elite of scientists and technicians for the greatest good of the greatest number. Fourier, dividing all history into a series of evolving stages to culminate in a perfect "harmony," with his bizarre analysis of the passions and his ideal "phalanxes," suggests a kind of demiurge straining to create a new world out of chaos. Doubtless the future is never predictable; but there are periods when the clash between future and past gives the present a strangely tentative quality, so that it cannot be taken for granted; and the Restoration, like our own period of today, was such a time.

What give the Restoration and the July Monarchy their supreme interest are the energy, the originality of their intellectual productions; and it was, after all, the peace maintained by the cautious political regime that permitted, in spite of a wavering censorship, this free flowering of genius, suppressed for so long by the magnitude of historical events. If we compare these later periods with the Revolution and the Empire in terms of creative activity, then they appear not as an anticlimax but as an emergence into daylight after a long dusk.

It is not merely that the Restoration produced a

number of men of genius or high talent in the fields
of literature, of history, of the various arts and sciences: there is everywhere a stir of energy, of curiosity
about the whole human enterprise and an eagerness to
see all of its manifestations as interrelated, as aspects
of a larger unity. Balzac and many others followed
with excitement the dispute between the two great
naturalists, Cuvier and Geoffroy Saint-Hilaire, because
of the latter's insistence, in spite of Cuvier's classifica-
tions, that beneath its variety animal life is essentially
one, descended from a common source. The progress
in the various sciences was leading men to "the belief
that there was a general scientific method that could
be applied to all fields of activity";[4] the exploration of
the past was impressing them with a sense of the continuity of history. As the period develops, writes
Charléty, it is more and more difficult "to make a
rigorous division between the various categories of intellectual manifestations. The reciprocal action of the
great currents of thought and activity becomes stronger
and stronger; the men themselves, except in a few extreme cases, are hard to classify."[5] One might take it
as a symbol of the age that when in 1842 a commission
was appointed to plan for the building of six railroad
lines radiating from Paris, it elected as its chairman
none other than Lamartine, whose name we associate
with such ethereal poems as "L'Isolement" and "Le
Lac," and whom Balzac satirized in *Modeste Mignon*
as the leader of "the angelic school" of poetry.

This was of course the period of the great romantic

[4] Frederick B. Artz, *Reaction and Revolution* (New York and London, 1945), p. 188.
[5] S. Charléty, *La Monarchie de Juillet* in *Histoire de France contem-
poraine* (ed. Lavisse; Paris, 1921), V, 349.

9

awakening. If young Frenchmen of the time turned with enthusiasm to Shakespeare and Sir Walter Scott, to Goethe and Beethoven (to mention only a few of their inspirations), this did not keep them from expressing with sharp originality their own temperaments. Alfred de Musset's first volume of poems appeared in 1829, the same year as *Le Dernier Chouan ou la Bretagne en 1800,*[6] Balzac's first novel to be signed with his own name. In 1830 the famous battle of Hugo's *Hernani* marked a victory for the new romantic drama over classical tradition, and Stendhal's publisher brought out *Le Rouge et le Noir.* In 1831 Delacroix sent six pictures to the Salon, and the next year Hector Berlioz returned to Paris from Italy where he had gone as winner of the *Prix de Rome.* History and fiction had never cast such a living glow upon each other. While novelists and dramatists were trying to recapture the air of earlier centuries, Michelet in his vast *Histoire de France* was portraying Louis XI and Joan of Arc, Thierry was relating the passionate deeds of "Hilperik" and Frédégonde, with the warmth and color of a first-rate historical romance. But more important than this fascination with the past (at least in the minds of the two greatest novelists of the period, Stendhal and Balzac) was the tendency to see the present itself as part of the historical process. The subtitle of *Le Rouge et le Noir* is *Chronique de 1830; Lucien Leuwen* is an ironic account of political life under the July Monarchy; and, as we shall see, *La Comédie humaine* is even more profoundly shaped and colored by the idea of the present as history.

6 To be reissued later in revised form, as *Les Chouans ou la Bretagne en 1799.*

Meanwhile the material life of the times was evolving in more prosaic fashion. Fortunes were made by speculation out of the ruins of a world blown to pieces; the little shops with their individual and often hereditary craftsmen were beginning to make way for the modern store (though Balzac was not to live to see the huge department stores that Zola describes in *Au Bonheur des dames*). "Business" was in the air: during the years of the Restoration the deposits in the Bank of France more than tripled; the great French bourgeoisie, with its various degrees and nuances, was coming into its own. Machinery had started to gather the momentum that was to change in a few generations almost every aspect of living more than it had changed in the last thousand years.

And yet until the end of the July Monarchy the physical background of daily life still suggested in many ways the *ancien régime* and even the Middle Ages; progress was more gradual in France than it was in England and America; people of every class clung to their traditions. Although the first French railroads, for example, began functioning in 1828, no one dreamed of the importance they would assume, except the utopian followers of Saint-Simon; and twenty years later, when the Monarchy was overthrown, there were only in the whole of France about 825 miles in use. Paris was far from being the great modern city we know; it was, in fact, barely more than a quarter as large as it is today. Passy and Montmartre were still country villages and the Bois de Boulogne was a mile beyond the city limits. It was during the Restoration that the first sidewalks were laid and that gas was first used in some of the principal avenues and squares. The

11

Galignani *Paris Guide* for the year 1819 speaks of the narrow dirty streets "in which not a ray of sunshine can penetrate the whole year round," and adds that "even the more noted streets in the central part of the town are constantly covered with a jet black dirt," though it does admit that "one may walk with clean shoes in the Tuileries, in the courts of the Louvre," and in a number of other select spots. Apparently conditions had not greatly improved by 1838, for the *Guide* of that year refers to "the black unwholesome gutters of the greater part of the central streets of the capital," which visitors reached by coach or cabriolet, by *calèche* or berline, or, if they preferred, on horseback.

As one tries to imagine as a whole the period of some thirty years from 1815 to 1845 that Balzac chiefly described, one pictures the cross section of an archeological digging which exposes a succession of cultures overlying each other—except that in such an excavation the layers are not mixed and there is no movement, whereas in the world Balzac knew each layer was mixed with all the rest in a bewildering jumble and nothing for a moment was ever still.

3

If Balzac's father came from peasant stock, the novelist's own family background as he was growing up was that of the liberal bourgeoisie, the class that more than any other was to set its mark upon the age; and Balzac was inside his age in a way that Stendhal and

Flaubert never were. Though Stendhal shows us a number of middle-class characters, the typical bourgeois plays a minor role in his novels. For Flaubert, the respectable bourgeois of a generation later is the smug pharmacist and freethinker, Monsieur Homais, the corrupt bohemianized bourgeois, Jacques Arnoux, the exploiter of artists, both magnificently presented, but described by an enemy. Now though Balzac was fascinated by the nobility, as he was by the world of the criminal and the prostitute, it is the bourgeoisie that plays the biggest rôle in *La Comédie humaine*. No one sees more sharply than he its greed, its stupidity, its lack of scruple; he, too, like Stendhal and Flaubert, observes it without illusions, but he is able at the same time to recognize its solid virtues. All through his life he kept the admiration and affection that as a boy or a young man he had formed for a group of older friends of his own class: Théodore Dablin, a wealthy hardware merchant; Captain Périolas, a former officer in Napoleon's army and a source of information for the projected novel, *La Bataille;* Dr. Nacquart, who gave expert advice about the formula for César Birotteau's marvelous skin lotion. The virtuous and charming Madame Carraud, for whose opinion Balzac had always the very deepest respect, was a liberal bourgeoise and proud of the fact.

But he not only kept many friends among the great middle class: with his craving for speculation, his active interest in business, he shared some of its enthusiasms. In 1825, as a short cut to wealth and power, he set up a publishing house. It was to bring him nothing but worries. He was staggered by a series of disasters—

the successive failures of the publishing business, a printer's firm, and finally a type foundry. The definitive collapse came in 1828, when he was saved from out-and-out bankruptcy only by the generosity of his mother and of Madame de Berny, and by the skill of a shrewd cousin who managed the liquidation of his affairs. From that time until the end of his life he was never out of debt.

This was not, however, because of his early failures alone, for he might have made good his debt with what he earned from his novels. It was partly the result of other speculations; but the true cause was his naive extravagance: he simply could not resist whatever appealed to him, whether it was clothes or books, pictures or antique furniture, a box at the opera or a house in the country.

Nearly ten years after his early ventures he tried to manage, almost without help, a magazine, *Chronique de Paris,* whose collapse after six months was equally disastrous. The next year he traveled to Sardinia in the hope of extracting by modern methods what silver might be left in the ore abandoned by the ancient Romans. Two years later he founded another magazine, *La Revue Parisienne,* which ran for only three issues and for which he himself provided nearly all the copy. He speculated for Madame Hanska, his future wife, in shares of the Chemin de fer du Nord; and when he visited her at her estate in the Ukraine three years before his death, he conceived the idea of shipping lumber from her forests into France and selling it at a profit. But if financial pressure was a constant worry, it was also a stimulus to work and a source of material.

14

It acquainted him with the world of moneylenders and creditors, with the desperation of young Rastignac when he writes for money to buy himself clothes that will not disgrace him in the Faubourg Saint-Germain, of César Birotteau when he faces bankruptcy. No one felt more than Balzac the shadow cast by the glitter of the times; and yet, if Balzac the observer was disillusioned from the start, Balzac the observed was never wholly disillusioned.

Politically, however, his views began to change about his thirtieth year, and soon he abandoned once and for all the bourgeois liberalism that had been the tradition of his family. Throughout the rest of his life, with minor shifts produced by political events and by new contacts with either people or books, he supported the royalist party and the Catholic Church. This change was no doubt partly prepared for by social ambitions, by a hint of snobbishness; but the more one examines its reflections in his writings, the more one is convinced of Balzac's sincerity and the less simple his views appear.

"Christianity," he wrote years later in his Preface to *La Comédie humaine*, "and especially Catholicism, being a complete repression of man's depraved tendencies, is the greatest element in Social Order."[7] This does not mean, however, that he was an orthodox believer. "I conceive of Catholicism as poetry," he wrote Madame Hanska. And again, more specifically: "I am not orthodox and do not believe in the Roman Church. Swedenborgism, which is only a repetition in Christian terms of ancient ideas, is my religion, though I should

[7] *Oeuvres complètes,* I, xxx.

15

add to that the incomprehensibility of God."[8] During the Restoration the doctrines of Emanuel Swedenborg aroused deep interest in certain Parisian circles,[9] and one can understand how they would appeal to Balzac and to the spirit of the times. Here was a man who—beginning his career as an engineer, mathematician, physicist, and physiologist—became a mystic and created a hierarchy of heavens and hells intimately "corresponding" to the material world in a unified system more grandiose than any of the social utopias. Though it has been suggested that Balzac knew his writings chiefly through a popular French digest,[10] they were to help determine the moral structure of *La Comédie humaine*. But if Balzac's views were heterodox and if he respected the Church partly for pragmatic reasons, he seems to have thought of it as an institution which, if fallible and transitory, was yet, in its stress on charity, brotherhood, and humility, the possessor of at least partial truth.

There is an ambiguity also in his political beliefs. Balzac was convinced that man needed an energetic government which could, if necessary, control him by force, and that the strongest government was the most unified.

Power should flow from a single source, as thought flows from the brain. It is akin to the power that runs the universe; it is a necessity of any social order. Absolute power is that which cannot be changed, either by those for whose profit it·is exerted, or by those who exert it. Arbitrary power is

[8] *Lettres à l'Etrangère,* I (1833–42, 3rd ed.; Paris, n.d.), 403.
[9] See Auguste Viatte, "Les Swedenborgiens en France de 1820 à 1830," *Revue de Littérature Comparée,* 11e année (1931), pp. 416-50.
[10] See Philippe Bertault, *Balzac et la Religion* (Paris, 1942), p. 364.

that which has the means of changing the conditions of its own existence. Such is the power based on election.[11]

The July Monarchy failed because of its democratic tendencies, its general flabbiness, and its distrust of youth. "Isn't it the most unlucky thing that can happen to a political party, to be represented by old men?" he asks in *Le Cabinet des antiques.*

But with Balzac, as some of his new legitimist friends suspected, it was the power, the energy that royalty once possessed which were important and not so much the fact of royalty itself. Writing to Madame Carraud in 1830, he compared Louis XVIII with Napoleon; and ten years later, in *La Revue Parisienne,* he put Napoleon in a class with Louis XIV, Charlemagne, and Saint Louis. It was not one of the French kings, but rather the Emperor himself, who stood for Balzac as the real symbol of power and energy.

Yet with all his apparent conservatism, and with a haunting fear of mob violence, Balzac kept a sharp sympathy for the underprivileged and the rebel. "Now when a government exerts its strength against the people," he wrote, "it is not the people that is wrong, but, in every case, the government, even when it is victorious. The gathering of any discontented group whatsoever is an act of accusation against the government, which should foresee its needs."[12] And this was not written during the liberal days of his youth, but appeared in *La Revue Parisienne* in 1840. He speaks of "the convict prison which hideously symbolizes the interest of the starved belly, the swift bloody protest of

[11] *Catéchisme social,* XL, 691.
[12] *Sur les Ouvriers,* XL, 407.

17

hunger!" When Abbé Brossette, the parish priest, suggests to a well-meaning chatelaine certain ways of improving the lot of the neighboring peasants, she replies "with the fatal *We'll see!* of the rich, which contains enough promises to let them brush off an appeal to their purse, and which allows them later to stand with arms folded before any misfortune, on the grounds that it has already occurred."[13]

Balzac never lost touch with his beginnings. He kept his freedom in regard to the royalist party as he did in regard to the Church. One can see how Marx and Engels and later left-wing critics, minimizing the importance of his bourgeois background and his acquired royalism, could feel that he was after all on their side. Balzac was interested in any social, political, or economic theory, whether from the right or the left. Certainly the Catholic traditionalism of de Maistre and Bonald, with its insistence on the supremacy of society over the individual, helped to shape his views in regard to both church and state. The all-embracing systems of Saint-Simon, of Comte, and of Fourier may have inspired him to apply to the field of the novel an equally original and comprehensive scheme.

4

Balzac, then, like many of his fellow citizens, was closely involved in the social and economic life of the age, and there is hardly a novel in *La Comédie humaine* that does not reflect this preoccupation. But he was,

[13] *Les Paysans,* XXIII, 220.

first of all, a creative artist and one may think of his social interests, profitable as they were to his genius, as in a sense peripheral, as furnishing a welcome escape from the exhausting road that his daimon compelled him to explore. It is a road that, sooner or later, every artist must travel alone; but Balzac was often encouraged, stimulated, and sometimes led astray by the example of past writers and by the effervescence of his contemporaries.

Like any French boy who has been through *collège* or *lycée,* he had read the French classics. Molière in particular remained an inspiration throughout his life; but it was to Corneille that he turned when, as a boy of twenty, he began the composition of *Cromwell,* a poetic tragedy. He had already spent two years studying law, attending courses at the Sorbonne, and helping in the offices of two of his father's friends—those offices with their mischievous young clerks, their dust and drudgery that we see later in *Le Colonel Chabert* and *Un Début dans la vie.* But soon he realized what his lifework must be. With his father's reluctant consent, he dropped his studies and lived for a year and a half on a very meager allowance in an attic in a dingy old quarter near the Place de la Bastille, struggling to prove to his family that he could write. *Cromwell* itself is wooden and immature. Still, when one reads the lines:

> But heaven created me to astonish the earth

or

> The thirst for power and renown
> Spurred on my rashness and had set it on fire[14]

---

[14] Balzac, *Cromwell* (texte inédit, ed. Walter Scott Hastings; Princeton, 1925), sheet 11.

19

one may fancy that the young Balzac, as he gazed out of his attic window across the roofs of Paris, caught for a moment through that magic air a signal of his future greatness.

Disillusioned with tragedy, young Honoré now turned to the novel. He wrote a fragment, *Falthurne,* the scene of which is laid in Naples in the eleventh century, and nearly finished a story set in modern Tours, *Sténie ou les erreurs philosophiques.* The style of both is heavily romantic. This is how Sténie, the heroine, describes the hero, whom she has seen swimming in the Loire:

His very beauty would be a handicap, if the pride that dwells in his eagle eye and on his brow did not proclaim him no woman; his skin is as white as mine; his hair is black. Why should I fear to confess to you that the roundness of his limbs, the elegance of his proportions, increased my love two-fold? I admired with fright his strength, the suppleness with which he cut the waves like a swan.[15]

And yet as we read on with a smile, we come upon this note by the fictional editor of the "correspondence": "It would have been easy for the most unskilled writer to delete the words: *Horribly, blackness, extreme, frightful, unheard-of,* which occur so often. But that would have been to alter the tone of each letter." In short, Balzac was not writing in his own style, but dramatically, in the style of his characters. This is a device he was to use many times in *La Comédie humaine.*

So far he had been trying, with whatever fumbling, to produce serious literature. The next novels, five of which appeared in the one year 1822, were written

[15] Balzac, *Sténie ou les erreurs philosophiques* (texte inédit établi par A. Prioult; Paris, 1936), pp. 57-58.

20

frankly to make money, and he signed his real name to none of them. In several of them he had the help of collaborators. His literary models here were chiefly the English novels of terror, which were having a great vogue in France, and the French popular novels of the late eighteenth and early nineteenth centuries. These included such works as Ducray-Duminil's *Victor ou L'Enfant de la forêt* (of which the most interesting passage is the invocation at the beginning of Tome III: "O you! famous German and English novelists, Werther, Goëther [*sic*], Schiller, come, come and strike my feeble lyre!") and, among the *romans gais,* the novels of Pigault-Lebrun.[16] But young Balzac had other, worthier examples. He was deeply excited by Sir Walter Scott, who became his early master in the architecture of the novel and who more than anyone else suggested to him the relationship between history and fiction; and during his twenties he read (in French) many other English novels. *Tristram Shandy* and *Clarissa Harlowe* were among his favorites.

The first of his series of potboilers, *L'Héritière de Birague,* is at once a novel of terror, in the tradition of Mrs. Radcliffe, and a parody of the genre. The book is scattered with satiric references to the nobility and the church. *Jean-Louis ou la fille trouvée,* the next to appear, is an example of the *roman gai.* In the midst of some rowdy fun and a good deal of claptrap, we come upon this sentence:

But I warn you that the most thorough knowledge of all these sciences will be of no use to you, if you have not *genius,*

16 The *roman gai* was a facetious and somewhat debased descendant of the picaresque novel; but if Pigault is often coarse and if his plots are quite irresponsible, he shows a breezy energy that suggests Smollett.

that is to say, if, out of thirty million men, you are not among the *ten* whom the whim of nature fashions so perfectly that your ideas are clear, accurate, new, and expressed by you in original phrases that paint with a word.[17]

There is no need to take up the next novels separately. In nearly every one Balzac was trying his hand at a different genre: the historical novel, the novel of terror (now taken seriously), the fantastic fairy tale (with a natural explanation), and at last the realistic novel in a contemporary setting. But if these books were pot-boilers, it is clear that Balzac was using them as exercises in the craft of fiction. *Annette et le criminel* (reprinted as *Argow le pirate*), by far the best of the series, did not appear until 1824. Its most surprising character is Monsieur Gérard, a retired government functionary. He might, just as he is, have stepped out of *La Comédie humaine*. To pass the time, now that he can no longer go to his office, he haunts the law courts to hear the trials; he listens to public lectures at the Sorbonne; he goes to the Louvre and the Museum of Natural History.

But the climax of his joy was when there was a good bowling match in the Champs-Elysées: he followed the players and balls with intense enthusiasm and yet an unlucky accident deprived him of this pleasure. One day, when he was sweating from having run with two intrepid players, it happened that the game had been so lively that all the ambulant spectators had finally given out. A stroke hard to decide came up and the two players both asking Père Gérard's opinion, he had to confess that he did not understand the game; so that he never dared come back to the bowling green.[18]

[17] "Jean-Louis" in *Oeuvres de jeunesse de Balzac* (Paris, 1879), p. 36.
[18] "Argow le Pirate" in *Oeuvres de jeunesse,* p. 3.

If I have gone into some detail in regard to a few of these youthful works, it is because without the training they gave Balzac, as he groped his way to his mature conception of the novel, and without the habit he formed as a young man of writing under pressure, one can hardly imagine his producing *La Comédie humaine*. It is through them, one might say, that the influence of his early reading was transmitted, so that it appears— at times unfortunately—in some of his greatest books. But sooner or later he read nearly everything that attracted his generation—Goethe, Shakespeare, Hoffmann, Cooper. One could extend the list indefinitely. The quantity of possible influences tends to cancel out the importance of each one. Balzac looked upon literature as he looked upon life; and, where his work was concerned, he hardly drew a distinction between them. It is not so much the influence of this or that writer, even among those to whom his debt is greatest, that colors *La Comédie humaine,* as the restless curiosity and energy of the age itself.

Le Dernier Chouan and *Physiologie du mariage, par un jeune célibataire* both appeared in 1829, the year after he had emerged from his youthful business disasters—shaking himself, out of breath, like a young retriever who has failed to get his bird. The novel did not arouse much attention; the *Physiologie* was a *succès de scandale*.

This was one of the great periods of the *salon;* people loved to meet at their friends' houses to talk of literature, of art, of politics—to discuss the swarm of ideas on every subject that kindled the air of Paris. Balzac began to attend some of these gatherings, the *salons* of Madame Récamier, of Baron Gérard (the painter), and of a number of others, where he met such people as Hugo and Stendhal, Cuvier and Delacroix. Over a hundred articles and reviews and, more important to us, the *Scènes de la Vie privée,* six long short stories, appeared during that year. In the meanwhile, as a financial venture, he had ghostwritten the greater part of the *Mémoires* of Sanson,[19] executioner of Louis XVI.

Balzac was dazzled by the worldly social life that was opening before him, as the young Marcel was to be some three-quarters of a century later; but he did not take the romantics and their admiring *cénacles* too seriously. Here is a fragment from an article in *La Mode,* for November 20, 1830, suggested probably by Hugo's reading of one of his own poems:

Sit down, the circle is formed. Now among all these attitudes, choose quickly whatever is most becoming, for you mustn't dream of sitting naively and simply. This gentleman who puts his elbows on his knees and hides his face in his hands, for fear lest a glance, a visible object should distract the deep attention which he is going to give the promised work; this lovely lady who with lifted brow and impatient eye fixes her eagle gaze on that poetic mouth which speaks so well of love; this friend who stands beside the reader and whose gesture imposes silence; and this last one, bolder and sometimes sublime, who lets all the chairs be taken, and forgetting himself in the midst of the circle, finally sits like a Spartan

[19] These are included in XXXVIII, 217-342, as "Souvenirs d'un Paria." Except for the original introduction, which Balzac used in *La Comédie humaine* as *Un Episode sous la Terreur,* a vivid scene in which Napoleon appears (pp. 222-27), and a few other short passages, they show the perfunctory style that one would expect of a work written under such conditions.

upon the floor—all these people know what their group expects of them.

Listen, listen, the reading begins! The silence of the desert, the immobility of the pyramids greet the first line of the elegy, or the ode, or the meditation, or the dithyramb.[20]

Surely the hostess must be Madame Verdurin.

One should not gather from this, however, that Balzac did not feel the impact of the romantic spirit that was sweeping Europe. Croce draws a distinction between "romanticism in the theoretic and speculative sense," a bracing revolt against the limitations of the purely academic and intellectual point of view, and "moral romanticism, romanticism as a malady." Although Balzac was by temperament quite out of sympathy with the plaintiveness and pallor of those who suffered from the *mal du siècle*,[21] *La Comédie humaine* is deeply colored by attitudes associated with what is most positive in the romantic movement—the sense of historical continuity, for example, and of the mystery that underlies the world of realistic appearances.

La Peau de chagrin and twelve *contes philosophiques* appeared during the summer of 1831, as well as nearly a hundred articles in the course of that year. Balzac was at last established; he was started on his period of almost incredible production. It is hard to give an exact idea of the task he performed, because he was constantly revising, sometimes combining shorter pieces

[20] *Des Salons littéraires et des mots élogieux*, XXXIX, 200.
[21] *La Comédie humaine* contains various satiric references to romantic affectations. See *Illusions perdues* (XI, 272 and XII, 102-3); *Modeste Mignon* (II, 56) and the whole treatment of the poet Canalis; also the description of Dinah's "romantic" period in *La Muse du département* (X, 72-73, 88-91, *et al.*).

to fit them into his general scheme (which was not called *La Comédie humaine* until 1842), and because even the first editions often went through so many re-handlings and enlargements while they were still in proof that the books we know are quite different from the original manuscripts. By the end of 1832 he had already published some thirty novels and tales which later became part of *La Comédie humaine,* and before his death he had added to these more than sixty others (some of them extremely long), the last twenty stories of *Les Contes drolatiques,* six plays, and about 385,000 words in miscellaneous articles.

In 1835, a very busy period, he wrote Madame Hanska: "One of my fiercest literary enemies used to say: 'Talent, genius, his incredible will power, I can understand it, I believe in it. But where and how does he find TIME?'" Of course without his phenomenal industry he could not have found it. "I have only a single good quality," he once wrote Madame Carraud, "it's the persistent energy of rats, who would gnaw through steel if they lived as long as crows." But this energy required discipline. He seems to have formed his well-known working habits in 1833, for in March of that year he wrote to Madame Carraud:

The machinery of my life has changed. I go to bed at six or seven in the evening, like the chickens; I'm waked at one o'clock in the morning, and I work until eight; at eight I sleep again for an hour and a half; then I take a little something, a cup of black coffee, and go back into my harness until four; I receive guests, I take a bath, and I go out, and after dinner I go to bed. I'll have to lead this life for some months, not to let myself be snowed under by my debts.[22]

[22] *Correspondance inédite avec Madame Zulma Carraud* (Paris, 1935), p. 136.

26

In October he described very much the same schedule to his sister and to Madame Hanska; and it was the one that, with interruptions and variations, he was to follow for years.

In several of his stories Balzac speaks of the excitement of working late at night. "What silence!" exclaims Ginevra di Piombo, who is coloring engravings to support her family. "Darling, I thoroughly enjoy staying up. The majesty of night is truly contagious, it overawes me, it inspires me. There is a mysterious power in this thought: everyone is asleep and I am awake."[23] And surely he was thinking of himself when, in *Les Proscrits,* he describes Dante working not on the *Human* but on *The Divine Comedy:* "Returning to his lodgings, the Stranger shut himself in his room, lit his inspiring lamp, and gave himself up to the terrible demon of work, seeking words out of the silence, ideas out of the night."[24] During those still hours Balzac wrestled, as few have done, with the demon of work; and, cut off from time by the circle of light about his desk, he must have lived more and more completely in that world which existed nowhere but in his own mind until, out of the silence and the night, from his own experience and his intuition, he created it for all men.

5

Balzac's attitude toward human experience was affected not only by the social and intellectual *climat* of the age, but also, inevitably, by his emotional relation-

23 *La Vendetta,* III, 213.
24 *Les Proscrits,* XXXI, 31.

ships with individuals. If his reading was extraordinarily wide and varied, so was the circle of his acquaintances. There is no room here to speak of most of them. There were, however, a few women who played such important rôles in his life that their influence cannot be overlooked.

"You take after your father in mind and spirit," Balzac's mother wrote him the year before his death; but if his energy, his curiosity, his bursts of optimism were a paternal inheritance, his lifelong and difficult relationship with his mother was doubtless even more important in determining his psychological development. When he was eight years old he was sent to boarding school, the *collège* of the Oratorians at Vendôme; he remained there for six years until April, 1813. During that period he rarely went home, and Madame Balzac, who preferred his younger brother Henry,[25] almost never came to see him. These years, on the whole, were bleak and wretched; it is not surprising that neither masters nor students felt at home with this rejected boy, the future creator of *La Comédie humaine*. But the most distressing thing for Honoré was not so much the hardships of school, as the sense of being deserted by his mother. This was to rankle in his mind as long as he lived.

Pretty, rather pert-looking, Madame Balzac was a fretful, practical-minded housewife with a taste for reading the mystics. In his early twenties Honoré wrote

[25] There is good reason to suppose that Henry's father was M. de Margone, a wealthy friend of the Balzac family, and consequently that Henry and Honoré were half brothers. Honoré's knowledge of this might help explain his attitude toward his mother. See Bernard Barbery, *En Marge de la Comédie humaine: Henry de Balzac; ou, Une double famille* (Paris, 1938).

of her as follows to his sister Laure: "She'd be the unhappiest of women if she suspected that when she thinks she's making those around her happy she's doing nothing of the sort. Mamma thinks a financial sacrifice counts more than a century of good humor."[26] The correspondence of mother and son over the years is full of alternate scoldings and affection: it is certain that she was proud of him and in her own way loved him; it is certain that he could not be indifferent to her. "And I was going to plunge bravely into my work when your letter arrived and completely upset me," he wrote in 1832. "Do you think I can have artistic thoughts when you suddenly give me such a picture of my wretched difficulties!"[27] But the next day he wrote: "After I wrote you yesterday, I fell into the most tender mood. Poor Mother! How can I repay you, when can I repay you, can I ever repay you in affection, in happiness, for what you do for me!" His feeling toward her seems to have been partly a deep sense of injury, partly a sense of guilt after he had written her harshly or ignored her, partly a real affection, or rather perhaps a sense of what that affection might have been under happier circumstances. In 1849 he wrote Laure from Poland apropos of a letter from his mother: "It was the letter of a mother to a little fifteen-year-old boy who has been naughty." But he added: "And with all that, my mother is completely devoted to my interests; she is taking my place and deserves nothing but praise."[28] It was on the whole a painful and compli-

[26] *Honoré de Balzac: Letters to His Family,* (ed. Walter Scott Hastings; Princeton, 1934), p. 41.
[27] *Ibid.,* p. 89.
[28] *Ibid.,* p. 296.

cated relationship, but perhaps not without profit for Balzac's genius. On the same day that he wrote his sister the passage quoted above, he wrote his mother:

I certainly don't ask you to make a pretense of feelings you don't have, and God and you know that you have never smothered me with tenderness or signs of affection since I was born. And you did well, for if you had loved me as you loved Henry, no doubt I should be where he is, and in that way you have been a good mother to me.[29]

The unclouded affection between him and his favorite sister Laure is a pleasant contrast.

How happy I should be, [he wrote her. in 1819 as he started work on *Cromwell*] if I should make the name *Balzac* famous! How wonderful to be remembered! So whenever I've caught a fine thought and put it into a sounding line, I think I hear your voice telling me: *Keep it up! Courage!* I hear the tones of your piano and I go back to my worktable with new eagerness.[30]

Far more important in his life than his feeling for his sister was his love for Madame de Berny and her complete devotion to him. He met her in 1821 at Villeparisis, a small town near Paris, where his family at that time was living. Nothing could be less romantic in appearance than their relationship. When the liaison began, she was forty-five years old and had borne ten children, eight of whom were living. She seems herself to have felt at first the absurdity of becoming the mistress of a man exactly the age of her third child, her oldest son, who had died seven years before. After the

29 *Ibid.*, p. 290.
30 *Ibid.*, p. 7.

affair ended, with her advancing age, their friendship continued until her death in 1836—the sharpest and most lasting grief that Balzac ever knew.

Her portrait shows us a face sensitive but not beautiful, with intelligent eyes set far apart and a rather hesitant smile. In spite of her childhood at the court of Versailles and the fact that her husband came from the old nobility, her own attitude was liberal and open-minded. She was a tactful and frank critic not only of Balzac's work but of his character. After objecting, for example, to two pretentious phrases in *Louis Lambert,* she remarked: "Make the whole crowd notice you, my dear, by the high place you have reached, but don't cry out to it for admiration." Two years after her death, he wrote of her to his sister: "I have no other guide than this inevitable thought: what would she say if she were alive?" Five years later he wrote Madame Hanska: "Since I never had a mother of my own, Madame de B. became my mother."

If the loneliness of his childhood deepened his understanding of all human loneliness and sorrow, drove him into himself and made him independent, the feeling of security that Madame de Berny gave him must have helped him to keep the sympathy, the courage, the exuberance that were such essential parts of his genius.

From the time of his first real success, in 1830, enthusiastic readers, especially women, began to write him, often under assumed names. It was in this way that he made the acquaintance of the two women who perhaps (with Madame de Berny) were the most important in his *éducation sentimentale*—Madame de Castries and Madame Hanska. Madame de Castries wrote him for the first time in the autumn of 1831, and her letter permitting him to call on her reached him in February, 1832, on the same day that he received the first letter (signed simply *L'Etrangère*) from Madame Hanska, the Polish countess whom he eventually married.

The Marquise (afterwards the Duchesse) de Castries belonged to one of the oldest families of the French nobility. She had been deeply in love with Prince Victor de Metternich, son of the imperial chancellor, and had separated from her husband. Victor had died three years before she met Balzac. At this time Balzac, dizzied by his first success, was trying (like several of the young men in his novels, Rastignac, de Marsay, Lucien de Rubempré) to cut a figure on the boulevards. He had a tilbury and a pair of horses; his clothes were made by a fashionable tailor. Although the Marquise was a beautiful and charming woman, part of her fascination must have come from her position in society. In *La Peau de chagrin* (written only a year before Balzac met Madame de Castries) the young hero, Raphaël Valentin, confesses: "An aristocratic woman and her subtle smile, the distinction of her manners and her self-respect delight me; when she puts a barrier between herself and the crowd, she flatters all the vanity that is in me, and vanity is half of love."[31] Eight months after their first meeting, Balzac's intimacy with the Marquise, though still platonic, had become so great that she invited him to go with her and her uncle, the Duc de Fitz-James, on a trip to Italy. The

[31] *La Peau de chagrin*, XXVII, 108.

break occurred in Geneva. Balzac wished to become her lover, and she refused to accept his conditions.

I have spoken here of Madame de Castries because many people have made the charge that Balzac did not know and could not describe the aristocracy. Certainly he had far more opportunity to know it at first hand than most novelists have had. The Marquise de Castries is said to have been the model, or one of the models, for the Duchesse de Langeais. It is chiefly through his friendship with her, the people he met and the houses he entered because of her introductions, that he came to know the great Parisian ladies who appear in his stories transformed into such characters as Madame de Beauséant or the frail Diane de Maufrigneuse.

Although the period of his closest friendship with the Marquise was less than a year, as long as he lived they occasionally saw each other and corresponded. Two years after their quarrel she wrote him:

Last night I was tormented by a cruel dream, and I feel an urgent need to come to you. My dear, one breaks with a mistress; but with a friend, a friend who would like to rejoice in all your happiness and share your sorrow, a friend of three years' standing who has shared your thought, a friend so sad and so ill. . . .[32]

In 1844 Balzac dedicated to her *L'Illustre Gaudissart* and in 1847, although she was then an invalid, she had herself taken to see the house he was preparing for his bride.

[32] *Correspondance inédite de Honoré de Balzac avec la Duchesse de Castries* (Paris, 1928), p. 24.

Madame de Castries presented him with a new field of material. Madame Hanska imposed her influence over all the latter part of his life, though even with her, until the last few years when illness and exhaustion had begun to sap his amazing energy, he kept his moral and intellectual freedom. Born Evelyn, Countess Rzewuska, she belonged to an ancient Polish family and lived with a husband twenty years older than she in a château on a large estate in the Ukraine. She was intelligent, restless, lonely. In her nature was a mixture of sensuality and mysticism that suggests a character from Dostoievski. She could be faultfinding and jealous; she could display the aggressive pride and also the condescension of a great lady who considers herself superior to her surroundings. A portrait shows her an opulent handsome woman with a pale skin, dark hair, and a serenely determined expression; whether one likes her or not, one must grant that she was a woman of strong personality.

After months of a more and more ardent correspondence, Balzac went to Neuchâtel in September, 1833, to meet her for the first time—almost exactly a year after his trip with Madame de Castries—and joined her in Geneva before Christmas to spend several weeks with her in the absence of her husband. They were now lovers, and they were often to meet again in France or abroad, in Austria, Italy, or Russia, sometimes after an interval of years, until they were married a few months before Balzac's death. Count Hanski had died in 1841. People have criticized her for not marrying Balzac at once; but it was a complicated business for a Polish heiress to settle a huge estate and marry a foreigner; she wished also, before committing herself, to arrange for her daughter's marriage. Perhaps she suspected that Balzac would not be a reassuring husband. If her delay caused him periods of loneliness, of impatience and distress, I doubt whether an earlier marriage would in the long run have made him happier.

As one reads through the *Lettres à l'Etrangère*,[33] one feels that with Madame Hanska Balzac was seeking, more than anything else, the security and comfort his first love had given him. After Madame de Berny's death, he wrote: "When I am wounded like this, I fly now only toward you, toward you who understand me and who judge me objectively enough to make your praise worth something." His letters are full of such expressions of confidence. "It means so much to me to know the security of being loved, to love as I do, with a power and depth that time alone reveals."

The pathos of the letters comes from the fact that this constant idealization demanded such an effort, that Madame Hanska did not and could not give him the exclusive devotion he wanted. They are saved from being tragic, however, by the exuberance of his nature, by the various sides of him she could not touch. Balzac, once in full possession of his genius, could stand quite alone. This series of letters—which cover as much paper as half a dozen novels—perfectly illustrates his faculty for seeing his own life, even when he is living most intensely, as itself a kind of novel. Whatever occupies him, there is always something that prevents his

[33] The title given to the four volumes of Balzac's letters to Madame Hanska.

being really caught; the one time he gives the whole of himself, without reserve, is when he is at work.

It is not only the Polish characters in *La Comédie humaine* (Wenceslas, Paz, Adam de Wierzchownia, and the rest) and the traces of her that may appear in his pictures of various women that Balzac owes to his relationship with Madame Hanska. His knowledge of the Polish temperament must have armed him against provincialism, and given a new dimension to his feeling for human nature and human destiny.

6

But what kind of man was he himself, Balzac the observed, the most immediate source of all his material? The facts of his life reveal his energy, his resilience, and his courage. We can form an idea of his extraordinary power of concentration from a letter written to Madame Hanska in 1836 at the height of his creative activity. He tells her of the death of Madame de Berny whom, as he truly says, he will never forget. At the same time he mentions a trip to Italy on some business for a friend. His own nephew has just arrived penniless in Paris, and Balzac and his mother must go to law to rescue him from the incompetent guardianship of his father, Honoré's brother Henry. His publisher of the moment, Madame Béchet, has brought suit against him because he has passed the deadline by which he was to give her two volumes; by agreement he must pay her fifty francs damages for each day's delay, and already he is two months behind. It is in the midst of this whirlpool that he has conceived the idea of the first part of *Illusions perdues* (*Les Deux Poètes*) and, in a week, written one-third of the book.

It is hard to generalize about him. If he would have liked to live, and for short times did live, as a sybarite, he lived far more often as an ascetic. The urge to fulfill his task might make him seem egotistical or even cruel, yet no one was more naturally kind; no matter what outrageous or apparently absurd things he did, he was able to keep throughout his life the love and respect of his old friends.

Everyone is familiar with his likenesses: the heavy shoulders, the round smooth neck, the full cheeks and rounded chin, the line of the moustache, the features rather small, perhaps, in proportion to the size of the face—a face which suggests intense mobility concealed under a mask of flesh, and which is dominated by the remarkable eyes. "As for his eyes," Gautier wrote, "there was never anything like them. They had an inconceivable life, light, magnetism." And Champfleury, years after Balzac's death, interviewing the aged doorkeeper at the school in Vendôme, reported that he still remembered "the great black eyes of Monsieur Balzac."

Many of those who knew him speak of his laugh, his broad jokes, the verve and charm transfiguring his face when he talked, as if it were lighted from within by all the joy, the good humor, the earthy, breezy health of the world. No one could lose himself more completely in the moment. No one at times could have more faith in his own genius. All through his correspondence we can feel his childlike pleasure in the book on which he is at work or perhaps has just finished: "Day after tomorrow they are publishing *Ursule Mirouët.* In my opinion it's the masterpiece of the novel of manners"; or, *"Les Bourgeois de Paris* is a masterpiece that makes everything look small in comparison. It's positively frightening in its verve, its philosophy, its originality, its vividness and its style." Sometimes he seems almost drunk with the size of *La Comédie humaine.* "You can't imagine what *La Comédie humaine* is! To compare literature with architecture, it's more immense than the cathedral of Bourges."

But there was another side which was just as really himself. Beneath his confidence there was anxiety. "What if I should not succeed? What if I should fall ill, in spite of the diet some doctors have arranged for me so that I can keep on working without risk? I've been ridden by a swarm of thoughts inspired by the seriousness of the things I am undertaking."[34] Or again, "I have no more strength, no more courage. The obstacles I used to take in my stride are now so enormous that they terrify me." If the spectacle of all experience fascinated and exhilarated him, it also filled him with horror and despair.

There is not only fear of the present and the future; there is discouragement with the past. In 1836, after the publication of *Eugénie Grandet, Le Père Goriot,* and numbers of other major works, he wrote Madame Hanska: "The month of May is approaching and I shall be thirty-seven; I am nothing yet; I've done noth-

[34] *Lettres a l'Etrangère,* I, 234-35.

ing complete or great." Two years after that he wrote: "There have been ten years of fruitless labor: the one sure thing is slander, insult, lawsuits, etc. You answer me with a lot of fine words; but I reply that any man has only a certain measure of strength, of blood, of courage, of hope, and mine is exhausted."[35]

There were moments, more and more frequent as he grew older, when he lost the ability to concentrate. "I've been here for a week, and for a week I've tried in vain to resume work. My mind refuses any intellectual work. I feel that it's full of ideas, and nothing will come out."[36] He thought at the end that he had not accomplished his task. "How different life looks when you're fifty," he wrote Madame Carraud the year before his death. "And how far we are from our hopes; Do you remember Frapesle, when I used to put Madame Desgrès to sleep? I've put to sleep a lot of people since then, I imagine, and would you believe it, except for my affection which is always growing, I'm no further ahead than I was."[37]

From his youth he was driven alike by the need for love and the need for fame. It may have been the impossibility of reconciling the two in the real world that forced him to create another where the jealousies, the loves, the ambitions of two thousand characters—most often thwarted, occasionally triumphant—were at the same time his own and not his own. But perhaps even greater than the need for love or fame was the need for action, for struggle. No matter how plausibly we may

[35] *Ibid.,* p. 468.
[36] *Ibid.,* p. 394.
[37] *Correspondance avec Madame Carraud,* p. 321.

weave theories about him, he always escapes through the meshes, just as he always escaped the people—even those he most loved—who wished to pin him down and make their special Balzac the only one.

PART II

The World of La Comédie Humaine

This magic prose not only evokes for us the river and its shore, the forests and their trees, but it does so by giving us, at one and the same time, the most minute details and the sense of the whole.

—Balzac's discussion of James Fenimore Cooper in *Lettres sur la Littérature*

1

As we read the works of any great novelist, we seem to be entering a special region through which the characters move and from which they take on a distinctive coloring that gives them all, no matter how various, an air of interrelationship, of existing within the frame of the same picture; just as a crowd of people moving out of doors is given a kind of visual unity by the overarching sky. We may think of this unique and personal region as the novelist's world. Though we could not have imagined it ourselves, once we have stepped across its border we are constantly reminded of it in the field of our own experience: the face of a man across the aisle from us in the train, the shadows in a street at night, may recall the Karamazov family or the Maison Vauquer; the buzzing quiet of a country town may suggest the air that surrounds the young Marcel and his Aunt Léonie, or the next instant, by some magic shift, the drier air through which Emma Woodhouse and her father and the magnificent Mrs. Elton so precisely move. It is background, but it is more than background. It is the shimmer of the sea at Balbec or the darkness of Egdon Heath; it is also the social framework in which every character is assigned his place, and its very existence implies a moral judgment which gives the actions of each one their significance.

To be felt as a world, however, it must have a certain size. There are, of course, great single novels: one thinks of *Adolphe, Les Liaisons dangereuses*, and

Wuthering Heights. Part of the greatness of the last two is the way in which their writers, within the limits of one book, have managed to suggest depth and extension; but even *Wuthering Heights* seems more the tantalizing fragment of a world than a world itself— like a marvelous and wild region which has been surrounded, just beyond the horizon, by the encroachments of a built-up section. You know you can walk only so far without coming to an end.

In some of these universes created for us by individual genius the light is so transparent, it reveals everything so subtly and exactly, that we may at first think of them as lacking depth or warmth. The reader must have lived for a while in Jane Austen's world to sense the hint of evil in the neatly brushed shadows, or the glow of spiritual integrity that is its counterpart. Then there are regions so crudely colored, obscured by such opacity of darkness, that on peering into them we are hardly aware of anything but mass and confusion. We draw back, disturbed by what strikes us as their arbitrary violence. But if we overcome our rather squeamish impulse, we soon discover the intensity of life, the highly personal art that are hidden beneath this surface excitement. Such are the worlds of Dostoievski, of Dickens, and of Balzac.

None is more dense, more filled with strain and pressure, than *La Comédie humaine.* Few give such an illusion of unlimited extent. As Henry James says in *The Lesson of Balzac,* "Quantity and intensity are at once and together his sign."

2

The center of *La Comédie humaine* is the city of Paris
—the main scene of more than half the novels and
stories. It is a mysterious realm, which—like a place in
a dream—may at one time seem to contract, to be
crowded together into a small space, a labyrinth in
which we have the feeling of walking again and again
along the same corridor without quite knowing how
we have reached it, but which suddenly may expand
into vistas or open to reveal depths. It is a city of end-
less variety; every quarter, every street has its own
character. Some streets are vicious, even criminal;
others are honest and hardworking; there are streets
that are always filthy, or always clean; there are, as
Balzac says, "streets that seem older than the oldest
dowager. In short, the streets of Paris possess human
qualities and we cannot shake off the impressions
they make upon our minds."[1] There are the bus-
tling lighted quarters: "the brilliance of shops as sumptuous as the salons of the nobles before 1789; the poem
of the window displays destroyed every evening, re-
created every morning."[2] But we are led more often
through the dingy byways where the *petits bourgeois*
live, the shopkeepers, the government clerks, the keep-
ers of cheap pensions with their mixed and dubious
boarders. Some of these quarters swarm with life, like
the region around the rue de Lesdiguières where Balzac

[1] *Histoire des Treize: Ferragus, chef des dévorants*, XIII, 13.
[2] *Gaudissart II*, XIX, 283.

45

himself had lived as a young man and where the blind old Facino Cane with his two blind comrades made music in the room above a wineshop. Some of them are ominously deserted, as if forgotten in the midst of the city: "There, the pavements are dry; the gutters have neither mud nor water; grass grows along the walls. The noise of a carriage becomes an event, the houses are gloomy, the walls suggest a prison."[3]

Raphaël Valentin looks from his garret window "over a landscape of roofs, brown, grayish, red, of slate, of tiles, covered with yellow or green moss. Sometimes in the evening, streaks of light from ill-closed shutters gave hints of life and color to the black depths of this peculiar country." He loves to watch "the poetic and transitory effects of light, the melancholy of the fog, the sudden sparkles of sun, the silence and magic of the night, the mystery of dawn, the smoke rising from the chimneys."[4] Or again, from a little hill near the Barrière d'Italie we gaze into the distance where "the gracious dome of the Invalides flames between the bluish masses of the Luxembourg and the gray towers of Saint-Sulpice,"[5] and Balzac tells how the sun can cleanse Paris, make its lines flow and its windows gleam, set fire to the golden crosses on its steeples, whiten its walls and transform it into a fabulous city of the Orient or the tropics.

But it is during the still hours of the night that we catch most sharply the sense of *Paris unanime:* a single throbbing unit.

[3] *Le Père Goriot,* VI, 223.
[4] *La Peau de chagrin,* XXVII, 98-99.
[5] *La Femme de trente ans,* VI, 128.

In the heart of Paris the last vibration of the last carriages returning from the ball has scarcely died away when already its arms are stirring at the gates and it shakes itself slowly. The gates yawn open, turning on their hinges, like the joints of a great lobster, all of them invisibly controlled by thirty thousand men or women. At noon it is alive everywhere; the chimneys smoke; the monster is feeding; it is filled with noise then, and its thousand claws tremble. But O Paris! who has not looked in wonder at your sombre landscapes, your vistas of light, your deep still alleys; who has not listened to your muttering between midnight and two o'clock in the morning has learned nothing yet of your real poetry, the sharpness and strangeness of your contrasts.[6]

Out of doors, in the streets and squares, among the damp shadows and uncertain light, the individual is in a manner lost—he assumes the color and tone of his quarter; but when he steps through his doorway and enters his own house, his own room, here he can impress himself upon his surroundings. In the Paris of *La Comédie humaine,* we are shown a whole gallery of rooms, each one the reflection of a person or of a family.

There is, for example, the apartment of Madame de Granville, with its anteroom "paved with black and white marble, decorated with a paper which imitated courses of stone," its intransigent dark-greens and purples and browns, as if Madame de Granville found lighter colors indecent. We see the shoddy luxury of the Marneffe ménage, the plaster statuettes painted to look like bronze, and Monsieur Marneffe's dirty socks trailing over the chairs in his bedroom; or the crowded

6 *Ferragus,* XIII, 15.

room of the widow Agathe Bridau where "the cats made themselves at home on the armchairs, the canaries, sometimes set free, dropped commas on all the furniture," where her late husband's pen is preserved in an envelope, with the label, "the last pen used by my dear husband." There are the sumptuous rooms of the fashionable courtesans, the boudoirs of the great ladies, the pretentious *salons* of the *nouveaux riches;* and then there are the attic rooms, filled with a breath of youth at once passionate and austere, "the cold garrets where great men without money live first when they come to Paris."

As we glance through this gallery of pictures, whether of rooms or streets, of squares or theatres or shops, we notice that Balzac rarely describes the particular aspect of the scene as it is affected by the day or the hour, or even by the season. There are, of course, scenes by night or by day; but they are, as a rule, generalized scenes—Paris during any night, Paris on any day. We could read through several of the Parisian novels and stories and scarcely remember whether it was summer or winter if the months were not mentioned here and there to inform us of the lapse of time. In *La Cousine Bette* (one of the longest), for example, which covers a period of nearly eight years, there is one mention of lilacs in bloom, but that is the only passage that calls attention to the time of year. Even in such panoramas as the view from Raphaël's window, it is not a single moment that Balzac is describing, but a permanent characteristic of the view—the way it is apt to change with the time of day.

This method of presenting Paris is different from

Flaubert's, as we find it in *L'Education sentimentale*.
It is through Frédéric's eyes that we watch the carriages returning from the Bois in the late afternoon
sunlight; it is through his mind that we feel the excitement of the dim sky, the rows of street lamps, as he
lingers late at night on the Pont Neuf. What Flaubert
gives are the light, the mood of the moment as seen and
felt by the characters involved. What Balzac shows us
are the places, the objects in themselves.[7] The streets,
the houses do not depend on the observer; they possess
a life of their own, an essential nature which is little
affected by the play of sunlight or shadow, by the cycle
of the changing year. The relationship between them
and the people whom they surround is not transitory,
but enduring—a relationship, one might say, of solid
objects rather than of light-bathed surfaces. These objects do change, just as the people change—in fact, we
have the sense that even the most massive, the most
fixed are always changing; but this change is not the
accident of the moment: it is the inevitable continuous
change of things in themselves that is the core of
history.

3

Moving through these streets, inhabiting these rooms,

[7] One must not exaggerate this distinction. There are scenes that Flaubert presents in themselves, without a spectator, such as the description
of Yonville-l'Abbaye at the beginning of the second part of *Madame
Bovary*. But such descriptions are rare in his novels, except in *Salammbô*,
where the city of Carthage and the movements of the armies are more
important than the individual characters.

are the masses of people who create the moral and social atmosphere of Balzac's Paris. Just as the streets intersect each other, just as some of them "have a fine head and end in a fish's tail," so the various social layers or "spheres" meet each other, tend often to merge, as people from the lower circles struggle to better themselves, or people from above sink into social decadence; but the lines of caste are none the less clear—even if they are often crossed—and we can best form an idea of this seething Parisian world by glancing at some of the separate worlds that compose it.

At the top is the *grand monde* of the aristocracy. Balzac's Faubourg Saint-Germain and Proust's Côté de Guermantes would seem to vouch for each other's genuineness by the striking way they suggest each other. If Balzac's duchesses may become involved in melodrama, if his presentation of them (as of all his characters) is shaped by his own temperament, I cannot help feeling that sometimes it is the critics who have a conventional idea of how duchesses behave.

In this world, as in Proust's, "to seek pleasure, is to find boredom. In Paris the rich are exposed to ready-made wit, predigested information and stock opinions which dispense them from having wit, information or opinions of their own."[8] The Duchesse de Langeais, who is presented as in many ways typical of the Faubourg Saint-Germain, is "a woman artificially informed, genuinely ignorant; full of fine feelings but without a thought to control them; wasting the loftiest talents in following the conventions."[9] Such women

[8] *Histoire des Treize: La Fille aux yeux d'or,* XIII, 334-35.
[9] *Histoire des Treize: La Duchesse de Langeais,* XIII, 190.

are apt to express their admiration "with that naive sprightliness, and those pretty transports of superficial friendship which captivate anyone who has not a thorough knowledge of Parisian life." For this very politeness is a kind of condescension, like that of old Madame de Villeparisis when she meets Marcel and his grandmother at Balbec. With each other there is a slightly different manner. When, for example, the Duc d'Hérouville ("courteous to every one, as a great lord is") meets his equal, the Comte de la Palférine, he uses "that special greeting which, while it implies neither esteem nor intimacy, is a manner of saying: 'We belong to the same race, the same family; we are equals.' "[10]

Their big parties can be brilliant and exciting, like the ball given by Lord and Lady Dudley which dazzles the outsider, Raoul Nathan; but what the clever ones prefer are the *salons intimes* after the crowd has left, where successful writers, artists, and diplomats may be admitted and where, "by a tacit and strictly observed convention," everyone forgets his self-importance. One of the pleasures of appearing at the opera, on the other hand, is precisely to revel in one's importance; like the Duchesse de Guermantes, the Countess Fœdora is delighted when, after scrutinizing the ladies in the other boxes, she convinces herself that she is the smartest woman there and can laugh at the awkward headdress of a Russian princess or a banker's daughter.

Always trying to push their way into this circle are the daughters and wives of the wealthy merchants and speculators, the newly rich of the Restoration and the

[10] *La Cousine Bette,* XVII, 447.

July Monarchy. Anastasie de Restaud, whose father made his money in vermicelli, has in a measure succeeded by marrying the Comte de Restaud; but she is still so insecure that her doors are closed to Eugène de Rastignac because he refers to her father. Her sister Delphine, wife of the banker Nucingen, is not so successful, although she "affected calling Mademoiselle de Grandlieu by her first name, as if she, née Goriot, frequented that society"; just as Madame de Gallardon makes a point of calling the future Duchesse de Guermantes "Oriane," to the latter's ironic amusement.[11] When Eugène gets Delphine an invitation to attend the ball of Madame de Beauséant, she is so excited that she puts off going to see her father in his desperate illness and shows the same heartlessness as her social superiors, the Duc and Duchesse de Guermantes, when their beloved friend Swann tells them he is doomed and they remain preoccupied with what slippers the Duchesse should wear to that evening's party.

If social ambition makes these women cruel, the men of the world of finance and big business are almost exclusively interested in money—money as a means of power. What attracts them is not the ballroom or the *salon* but the Bourse, "where the worth of kings is quoted on the stock exchange, where peoples are weighed, systems judged, and governments rated in terms of the five-franc piece."[12] No such relatively fixed line can be drawn between them and their less successful competitors as between them and the Faubourg Saint-Germain. The banker du Tillet began life

---

[11] I was interested to see that Proust refers to this very passage in *Le Balzac de Monsieur de Guermantes* (Neuchâtel et Paris, 1950), p. 76.
[12] *Melmoth réconcilié*, XXVII, 366.

as a foundling and later was a clerk in César Birotteau's business. The great bankers and the great moneylenders, such as Gobseck and Elie Magus, like the shabby Cérizet whose business is short-time loans, all take part in the same "continual battle between creditor and debtor." Utterly cynical where their business interests are involved, they can bring about a major failure, drive to desperation an indiscreet wife as she tries to pay her lover's debts, or ruin the existence of some petty clerk and his family.

We breathe a healthier air when we turn to the world of commerce. We respect Monsieur Guillaume and his honest clerk Joseph, who run the drygoods store at the sign of Le Chat-qui-Pelote. Monsieur Goriot is not only honorable, like Monsieur Guillaume, but capable of intense feeling; no one could be more honest and kindly than César Birotteau, and both he and Père Goriot are given depth and stature by the way they meet misfortune. For such men, however, the world of the arts, and of the mind generally, does not exist. César Birotteau's beliefs suggest the *idées reçues* that Flaubert loved to collect. Famous actors and actresses such as Talma and Mlle Mars

were multimillionaires and did not live like ordinary human beings: the great tragedian ate raw meat, and Mlle Mars sometimes had pearls fricasseed to imitate a famous Egyptian actress. Writers, artists died in misery as the result of their freakish behavior; they were moreover all atheists who should on no account be received into one's home.[13]

The difference between Flaubert and Balzac is that

[13] *César Birotteau*, XIV, 43.

Balzac realizes that the complete Philistine—stupid and in many ways absurd—may be a man of character, may even, if circumstances arise, achieve a kind of grandeur. When we turn from shopkeepers to professional men also of bourgeois background, to Dr. Bianchon or the admirable lawyer Maître Derville, for example, we often meet the same sense of honor, the same human kindness, without the intellectual limitations.

There is also among the Parisian bourgeoisie the rather special world of the petty clerks, the government functionaries that Maupassant was to describe fifty years later in *L'Héritage*. Like all the others, it has its subdivisions; and here they are determined entirely by the question of salary: there is the arctic region, with salaries not over 1200 francs, the temperate zone from 3000 to 6000, and throughout all zones "a kind of involuntary, mechanical, instinctive respect for that Grand Lama of every ministry, known to the clerk by an illegible signature and by the title of HIS EXCELLENCY THE MINISTER."[14] But for the functionary of whatever rank, "nature consists of the office. The weather for him is the air of the corridors, the reek of men shut up in unventilated rooms, the smell of pens and papers."[15]

Recruited from the bourgeoisie, but breaking with their traditions and creating a closed world of their own, are the writers and journalists. The few first-rate writers, Daniel d'Arthez, for example, or Claude Vignon, are uncorrupted by it; but the majority of

[14] *Le Père Goriot,* VI, 391.
[15] *Les Employés,* XIX, 120.

journalists, critics, and even poets and novelists are tainted by its cynicism, its malice, and its vanity—and the greatest of these is vanity. "No words, no description, can give an idea of a writer's fury when his vanity is injured, or of the energy he displays the instant he is pricked by the poisoned dart of ridicule."[16] Every writer hates and fears his colleagues if he thinks they are apt to be more successful than himself, and takes the most intense delight in watching "the death agony of one of his equals guilty of having tried to become his master." On the other hand, the opportunist critic Raoul Nathan is glad to praise a short story by the Comte de la Palférine, because he is sure the Count will never publish anything else.

When a writer has "lost all ability and all desire to amount to anything," he becomes *un homme de métier,* a reviewer and journalist. It is sometimes wise to write one's fiercest attacks anonymously, though of course you sign any flattering articles. To puff the sales of a friend's book or to purchase a return favor, you may even write a couple of articles (under different names) attacking, counterattacking, to arouse discussion, but end by proclaiming that it's "the greatest book of the age." As Blondet tells Lucien de Rubempré, "It's as if you said nothing at all. People say that of any book." Of course you may sometimes be under the necessity of damning a book that you know is first rate, but you can take that in your stride. "My dear fellow," Lousteau remarks to Lucien,

a journalist is an acrobat. You must get used to the drawbacks of the profession. You start by praising the book. The

16 *Illusions perdues,* XII, 322.

public will say: "This critic shows no signs of jealousy; he must be impartial." From then on, the public will assume that your criticism is sincere. Once you have won your reader's esteem, you will regret having to blame the tendency that such books are introducing into French literature.

Then various damning comparisons with past works of genius, or with obscure foreign writers ("There's nothing that establishes a critic like referring to an unknown foreign author"), a few solemn generalities (such as, "Animation is not life, description is not thought!"[17]) and the trick is done.

Closely connected with the world of journalism is the world of the stage. This too is a milieu without glamour. "In these filthy corridors cluttered with machinery, in the smoke of the oily lamps, there lurks a kind of plague that destroys the soul. Life there is no longer sacred or real. Anything serious is laughed at, and the impossible seems true."[18] Actors lead a hard life which in no way resembles the layman's idea of it. The days of Florine, for example, a second-rate but moderately successful actress, are filled with a monotonous and exhausting routine: rehearsals, performances, studying new rôles, arranging for her claque, taking measures to defeat any cabal which, in the interest of some other actress, may have been planned to cause her failure. Talent is not enough to win success. It may even be a drawback if it is not supported by a gift for intrigue, an ability to compromise, to put one's career ahead of everything else.

The dirtier fringes of the worlds of journalism and of the stage may sometimes merge into the ominous

[17] *Ibid.*, pp. 229-30.
[18] *Ibid.*, p. 167.

shadow of prostitution and crime—the world of the prison, the public hospital, and the police court. Most of the prostitutes in *La Comédie humaine* have adopted their career because of poverty, lack of work, or the treason of a first lover. "Going to extremes in everything, in their moments of joy or despair, in their religion or their irreligion, almost all would go mad if it were not for their especially high death rate or the lucky chances that lift some of them out of the mud in which they live."[19] Often they possess the virtues of frankness, generosity, and good humor. The most cynical, and therefore the most dangerous, are the married courtesans—like Madame Marneffe—who, trading on their alleged respectability, "accept depravity and all its consequences, determined to make money out of pleasure," under the shrewd direction of their husbands. The world of crime is dominated by the figure of Vautrin. We glimpse a tangle of loyalties and betrayals, of jealousies and homosexual attachments, in which it is hard to draw a line between the criminal and the secret police, the turncoat and spy.[20]

There remains a world, beyond all the others, from which the criminal and the prostitute are often recruited—the world of the people. In *La Comédie humaine* it is represented by few important characters. Now and then such a man as Philippe Bridau or Colonel Chabert, who come from another sphere, may sink into its shadow; there are also sharply drawn sketches, like those of Madame Cardinal, the

[19] *Splendeurs et misères des courtisanes,* XV, 39.
[20] For years Balzac was a friend of Vidocq, criminal in his youth and then police detective. In Vidocq's memoirs, ghostwritten but based on material furnished by himself, the use of thieves' cant, the allusions to homosexuality in the prisons, etc., suggest the documentation he must have given Balzac.

fishwife from the Halles, or Poupillier, the ex-soldier and -model; but as a rule the people are presented in nameless groups, like the crowd of clients who throng Judge Popinot's rooms—sick, brutalized by privation, avid for charity—or "the stinking squad of claqueurs and ticket sellers, in aged trousers, threadbare coats, with their gallows faces, their fierce and wheedling eyes, that lives and swarms on the boulevards." This very anonymity gives a sense of shifting crowds at once pitiful and frightening: it is as if the mud and fog of the Paris streets, like the fabulous slime of the Nile, had spontaneously given birth to life; as if anyone, no matter how prosperous or secure, might through his own vices or misfortunes be pulled down into that mud, to be stifled or permanently stained by its corruption. "Poverty," Balzac wrote in *Les Petits Bourgeois*, "has unfathomable depths, especially in Paris, like the ocean's slimy bottom, and when a drowned man floats back to the surface he brings up with him bits of filth sticking to his body or to his clothes."[21] Something of Villon's Paris survives in the Paris of Balzac, just as something of Balzac's survives in the sombre poetry of *Les Fleurs du Mal*.

4

All these worlds are divided within themselves by social nuances. In each there are characters who are far from typical. Nobody could show a greater contrast to

[21] *Les Petits Bourgeois*, XX, 82.

the sordid crowds of the people than the kind and self-respecting water carrier Bourgeat, who helped Dr. Desplein in his student days. There are various groups I have not mentioned—the young men about town, for example, de Marsay, Rastignac, Maxime de Trailles—because they cut across several strata. There are the very special worlds of Madame de La Chanterie and the Brotherhood of the Consolation, or the rowdy *confrèrie* of traveling salesmen (whose base is also Paris) illustrated by the great Gaudissart, or the world of the artists' studios where we meet Joseph Bridau and Mistigris; there are still others. And each one, directly or indirectly, flows into all the rest; each shade, blending with the next in a continuous play of light and shadow, is part of the sombre iridescence of Balzac's Paris.

But when we observe it as a whole, certain hues stand out. We have again and again the picture of Paris as a kind of hell, a city of masks—each one stamped with breathless greed, each one seeking for money and pleasure. Its language "has only two rhythms: self-interest or vanity." Nothing is sacred. Even death is an excuse for a swarm of profiteers—the undertaker, the seller of cemetery lots, and their tragi-farcical cortege—to come buzzing around the corpse. In its bitter and brilliant contrasts between wealth and poverty, honesty and vice, in the fever of its variety and the multiplicity of its temptations, it is "the heir of Niniveh, Babylon and imperial Rome." It is both a jungle and an Arabian Nights city in which anything may happen. "You cannot imagine the number of secret adventures, of forgotten dramas in this City of Sorrow!" exclaims the narrator, as he describes his wanderings through

59

the streets in *Facino Cane.* The famous Lawyer Derville says that his profession leads him through sewers which nothing can cleanse and that "all the horrors which the novelist thinks he is inventing fall short of the truth." The old-clothes dealer, Madame Nourrisson, "heard dreadful tales by getting her customers to talk about each other."

Even the streets offer the observer "a continuous free show." Loafers, "their faces branded by debauchery, seem to reproach you by their silence; their attitudes reveal grim thoughts. Each one has his dream, his hope, his pleasure: gambling, the lottery, wine."[22] But it is not only the sordid that disturbs our imagination: it is the mystery of the human face in the moving crowds, the glimpse that enthralls for a moment and is gone.

Who has not met on the Paris boulevards, at a street corner or under the arcades of the Palais Royal, some being, man or woman, whose sight fills our minds with a swarm of confused ideas? We are suddenly interested either by the strange modeling of a face in which we read the signs of a stormy life, or by the queer over-all effect of the gestures, the walk, the clothes, the manner; by the depth of a caught glance, or by something, we cannot say what, which strikes us swiftly and sharply without our being able to explain the cause of our emotion.[23]

Several of Baudelaire's poems—in verse or in prose —might have been inspired by such passages.

But Paris is also the city of light. "Ideas are in the air; they smile at you from the street corners; they

22 *Ferragus,* XIII, 42.
23 *Ibid.,* p. 146.

spurt up in a splash of mud from beneath the wheels of a cab!" As Lucien de Rubempré, fresh from Angoulême, writes his sister Eve: "You learn more chatting in a café or at the theatre in half an hour than you can learn in the provinces in ten years." No matter how much Paris might disgust or frighten Balzac, he could not for long live anywhere else; and it was not only the fascination of its strangeness, the multitude of its dramas that held him. Beneath his horror, his irony, his moral condemnation, there was a passionate love and pride, such as Isaiah—even as he cursed her—felt for Jerusalem. The streets of Balzac's Paris are often obscure; the thick air may press about you at moments as in a bad dream; but that air is also sacred. "There is in Paris," he once wrote Madame Hanska, "an air that you can find nowhere else, an air full of ideas, full of entertainment, full of wit, saturated with everything delightful and amusing; then a grandeur, a freedom that uplift the soul."[24]

5

In *La Comédie humaine* the influence of Paris reaches far beyond the city borders. It is the failure of the Parisian banker, Monsieur Grandet, that sends his son to Saumur, and it is partly this young man's Parisian elegance—so unlike anything she has seen before—that fascinates poor Eugénie and lays the foundation for her struggle with her father. The drama in *Mo-*

[24] *Lettres à l'Etrangère*, II, 106-7.

deste Mignon, which is centred in Le Havre, depends on Modeste's correspondence with the Parisian poet Canalis; Dr. Benassis, the country doctor, is started on his career by an early indiscretion in Paris. However, the comparison between the two ways of life, Parisian and provincial, intertwined as they are, emphasizes the differences between them; and the world of *La Comédie humaine* includes a large number of country towns, each with its own closed little sphere of interests, rivalries, and frustrations.

If in Paris we are in a man-made region where even the seasons are forgotten, these provincial towns are nearly always pictured in their natural setting: Guérande beside its salt marshes reaching to the sea, Sancerre on the highest peak of a ridge along the Loire which fertilizes the lowlands with its yellow mud, or Fougères built partly on a great rock overlooking a valley and a wide circle of hills. Sometimes we are given a topographical sketch of the town or village. Issoudun and Fougères, Angoulême and Arcis, with their different sections and something of their history, are presented in a detail that suggests an architectural print— or perhaps an ancient map on which the seas are peopled with ships and whales, and the continents with trees or animals or natives. Most of the towns are old, like Paris, but unlike Paris they show little contrast with the modern. Here there is neither noise nor movement. Describing Arcis, Balzac writes: "Nothing can explain provincial life better than the silence which enfolds this little town and which prevails in its most lively quarters."

As for the houses, if some of them show the stamp

of their present occupants (like the Rogron house in Provins, with its red and gold wallpaper, its stairway painted to imitate marble, and its big foolish lion on top of the clock), more of them have remained unchanged for a century and reflect the traditions of the family and of the place rather than of the generation that is passing through them. In the ancient Gothic house of the du Guénics the mantelpiece in the dining room has been "modernized," but this was done during the reign of Louis XV. Mlle Cormon's house in Alençon was built in the reign of Henri IV and has always been in her family. "What peace! What calm!" Balzac exclaims. "Nothing pretentious but nothing transitory: everything here seems eternal."

Outside the towns, scattered through the open country, we are shown a variety of houses, and most of these, too, are old. There are the châteaux: the manor of Montcontour, for example, "one of those little châteaux in Touraine, white, gracious, with its carved turrets, embroidered like Malines lace"; or the truly royal château of Les Aigues, of fine red brick, stone-trimmed, among its gardens and pools. In sharp contrast are the stinking hovels of the peasants, and between such extremes are all manner of villas and farms. There are also the deserted or partially deserted houses: the Grande Bretèche of sinister memory, or the crumbling priory in *Adieu* in its tangle of neglected orchards. Balzac's houses, like his people, are living entities; they have their shifts in fortune, the vigor of their prime, their old age, their gradual dissolution. Even Mlle Cormon's house seems eternal only in comparison with the swifter passing of its occupants; we feel that the stones of the sturdiest châteaux, built centuries ago and outliving generations of men, will at last return to the earth from which they were quarried. In Paris old houses are torn down to make room for new streets or shops. In the provinces it is the rain and the mildew that slowly overcome them, the stubbornness of the probing ivy, the roots of the wild flowers and grasses that bloom in the crevices of the tiles.

For here, where even the townsmen live close to woods and fields, the seasons are not forgotten. In *Les Chouans* the Breton landscape—its sunken roads, its blocks of granite, its fogs through which the trees loom "like branches of coral in the depths of a calm sea"—becomes a symbol of the primitive fierceness of the inhabitants. In *Le Médecin de campagne* we are given a clear picture of the upland fields and farms, the poplars rippling in the oblique sunlight, the granite cliffs partly covered by the blackness of the pines. Since the center of the novel is the contrast between Benassis' early defeat in Paris and the constructive manner in which he has found compensation, it is important that we should believe in the region's physical reality—it is, one might say, a kind of anti-Paris. It is for much the same reason that in *Le Curé de village* we are shown the wilderness around Montégnac. It is through its reclamation, the turning of it into fertile farmland, that Véronique at first is able to go on living after the shock of her lover's execution and, ultimately, with the help of the Abbé Bonnet to find spiritual peace. At his suggestion she starts out to explore the wild, thickly wooded hills of her domain. She is deeply moved by "the crushing sense of Nature's permanence," and by identifying herself with the scene around her she catches for a moment some hint of divine consolation. Yet even in the provinces it is the people, the drama that count; and as in the Paris stories, the real background against which they move is not the permanence of nature, but the flow of human history.

Occasionally Balzac goes, as it were, beyond history to give us a suggestion of the continuity of all life. In the forests of Les Aigues, Blondet and the Comtesse de Montcornet discover a pool where they watch the frogs, the lizards, the snails, and "the green stains on the water which are worlds in which life is forming." Félix de Vandenesse speaks of these same green stains ("a kind of transition between plant and animal, where life is born from one day to the next") which scum the ponds where plants and insects are floating "like a world in space." Fleeing from the cruelty of society, Raphaël Valentin comes upon an extinct volcano in the mountains of Auvergne. "When the sun poured down into the old crater, filled with water by some antediluvian cataclysm, the rugged sides became heated, the dead volcano took fire, and its swift warmth awakened seeds, fertilized plants, colored flowers and ripened fruits."[25] Under the direct sunlight, rocks and leaves, the sleek hides of animals, the wings of insects take on a special luster and appear like brilliant facets of one continuous whole. In such passages Balzac's style becomes flushed with an excess of color (as a rule, even in his landscapes color words are used sparingly); we feel a blast of warmth as if from a primeval swamp.

[25] *La Peau de chagrin*, XXVII, 273-74.

Related to these is the labyrinthine description of the flowers, "that diffuse torrent of overflowing love," which Félix gathers for Madame de Mortsauf. To me this passage is not an exercise in sentimental rhetoric, as it has sometimes been called, but rather the crude and tormented expression of a kind of Dionysiac "illumination." It suggests the flowers of which the young Rimbaud was to dream:

> Trouve, aux prés fous, où sur le Bleu
> Tremble l'argent des pubescences,
> Des Calices pleins d'Oeufs de feu
> Qui cuisent parmi les essences!
>   "Ce qu'on dit au Poète à propos de fleurs"

6

In the provinces the line between the nobles and the bourgeois is drawn as strictly as in Paris; and yet, because in each town the stage is so much smaller, the people of the different classes know each other, or at least know about each other. "With the exception of a few local customs, all little towns are alike," Balzac writes in describing Bayeux. At the top of the social scale there is the family of the oldest nobility, related to the great families of Paris but unknown beyond its particular small realm. "It clings to bygone fashions in silverware, furniture, carriages, as well as in manners and speech. This ancient pomp, moreover, fits in nicely with provincial thrift."[26] For this family is

[26] *La Femme abandonnée*, IV, 258.

often, like the du Guénics of Guérande or the d'Esgrig-
nons of Alençon, distinctly poor, though it has a naive
faith in the fortune that awaits its heir when he goes
to present himself at the court of the Restoration.
Around this family are grouped several others, often
wealthier but of less ancient stock—a few priests, and
a very few of the richer bourgeois, if their opinions are
suitably royalist. The level of intelligence is not high:
political discussion is a series of banalities in which
Louis XVIII is referred to as a Jacobin; the same ideas
are repeated endlessly, "like the rise and fall, the perpetual eddying of the tide." The women are without
real elegance, yet there is more nobility of feeling than
in the fashionable circles of Paris. This society is like
"a set of old-fashioned silverware, tarnished but massive. The immobility of its political opinions might be
taken for loyalty. The distance kept between it and the
bourgeoisie, the difficulty of breaking into it give it a
certain counterfeit dignity and a conventional importance."[27] These provincial nobles treat their inferiors
with the same overwhelming politeness as do the ladies
and gentlemen of the Faubourg Saint-Germain; but if
they do come to Paris, like Madame de Bargeton (a
leader of Angoulême's aristocracy), their provincialism
is at once obvious.

Beneath this circle there may be a group composed
of the richer and more established bourgeoisie—the
clergy, the magistracy. In actual affairs it exerts more
influence than the carefully guarded *salons* of the
nobles.

[27] *Illusions perdues,* XI, 221.

The wit and intelligence of the district are to be found in this solid unpretentious group, where everybody knows his neighbor's income and nobody cares about either luxury or dress. Unshakable in its prejudices, whether good or bad, it follows a single track, looking neither backwards nor forwards. It has no use for novelties; it never reads; it is totally blind to science, literature or industrial progress.[28]

Such is the *salon* of the charming and pathetic Mlle Cormon in *La Vieille Fille*. Far below this would be the *salon* presided over by Madame Soudry, former lady's maid of a local châtelaine, where we find the same self-satisfaction, more malice, and no touch of distinction. The further we descend in the social scale, the less fixed are the barriers between one circle and the next—until we come to the peasants who farm the surrounding country. Between them and even the smallest shopkeeper there is a barrier as great as that between noble and bourgeois.

The peasants and the workers are the two classes with which Balzac was least familiar. His peasants have kept something of the primitive misery of La Bruyère's. They live in a state of open promiscuity: "I must explain," he writes in *Les Paysans,* "to people accustomed to the morality of bourgeois families that the peasants have no delicacy whatever in their domestic habits; if one of their daughters is seduced, they invoke moral law only if the seducer is rich and timid. Their children, until the state conscripts them, are just so much economic capital."[29] They may display a callous savagery; but their behavior, like that of most

---

[28] *La Vieille Fille,* X, 298-99.
[29] *Les Paysans,* XXIII, 56.

people, depends upon the way they are treated. If the clumsiness of General Montcornet brings out all their worst traits, Dr. Benassis' understanding has the opposite effect. "I've never regarded my people romantically," he tells Genestas. "I've accepted them for what they are, poor peasants, neither wholly good nor wholly bad, for whom constant toil has left no leisure for sentimental indulgence, but who can feel deeply. At last I've come to realize above all that I can influence them only by taking into account their immediate interests and well-being."[30]

The peasants of *La Comédie humaine* have then a life of their own. The one novel in which they play leading rôles is the remarkable but uncompleted *Les Paysans*. There are sharp glimpses of them in *Le Médecin de campagne, Les Chouans,* and two or three other stories; but in the *Comédie* as a whole they appear rarely. La Grande Nanon is of course of peasant stock, and in her devotion and her admirable patience is one more example of the fact that throughout Balzac's work there are exceptions to every rule. Even in the fierce and depraved peasant milieu of the Tonsards we meet old Niseron, who had been president of the local Jacobin Club during the Revolution, "concentrating in his own person the integrity of the commune—hard as steel, pure as gold."

In the towns, however, aristocratic and bourgeois milieux show a number of common characteristics. These are the results of the narrowness and monotony of provincial life. "In the provinces a truly original man is considered half crazy." For to be original "is to

---

[30] *Le Médecin de campagne*, XXIV, 39.

possess ideas that other people do not understand, and they insist upon conformity of mind as well as of manners." The arts are looked upon with a mixture of condescension, boredom, and disapproval; "thought is persecuted by a brutal indifference." When Ursule Mirouët plays the piano before a group of her envious relations, the local tax collector explains:

"She says it's by Beethoven, who's supposed to be a great musician. He has quite a reputation."
"Well he certainly hasn't in Nemours," replied Madame Cremière.

Grudges are harbored for years with a persistence and an intensity that "would amaze diplomats who have learned to be amazed at nothing." The main field of interest is one's neighbor's affairs, which are scrutinized with an insatiable and often malicious curiosity. Life is based on a system of "meticulous espionage." When the good bourgeoise Mlle Cormon unexpectedly returns from her farm to Alençon and sends her cook to market to buy delicacies for a guest, the whole town wonders about it, even Mlle Armande who belongs to the nobility. Madame Mollot, in *Le Député d'Arcis,* carries her curiosity to the same lengths as Marcel's Aunt Léonie: "As soon as a peasant entered the square from the Brienne highway, she'd look at him and try to find out why he could have come to Arcis; she did not have a moment's rest until her peasant was explained."[31]

Since privacy then does not exist and originality is

31 *Le Député d' Arcis,* XXI, 355–56.

taboo, we can understand why people of imagination and talent often desert their native towns for Paris.

7

Yet beneath its variety, Balzac's world is one. The more intimately we know his characters, the more differences of caste and milieu tend to evaporate—revealing the differences of individual temperament and at the same time the traits common to all of Balzac's humanity. "Between Flore Brazier [the peasant mistress of Monsieur Rouget] and a duchess, between the duchess and the richest bourgeoise, between the bourgeoise and the most sumptuously kept woman, the differences are only those caused by their upbringing and the milieux in which they live," he writes in *La Rabouilleuse*.[32] He compares the jokes of the Parisian *salon* with peasant humor: "The subtle and the witty replace the vivid and the crude, that's the only difference." There are other such remarks; but the important thing is that Balzac is showing us these resemblances on almost every page of *La Comédie humaine*.

In every milieu there are characters engaged in a fierce and exciting battle. Often it would seem to be with other characters, individual against individual;

[32] *La Rabouilleuse,* IX, 428. "*Rabouiller* is a popular term in the region of . . . Issoudun. It has been (and still is) in current use. Only it has a wider meaning than Balzac seems to believe. . . . *Rabouiller* is applied to any action that clouds a liquid by stirring it."—Romain Guignard, *Balzac et Issoudun* (Issoudun, 1949), p. 72. Balzac defines the term (IX, 390-91) as clouding the water of a stream with a branch to frighten crayfish into a net.

but it is never solely that. No protagonist can be separated from the swarming social background of which he is a part; no individual can make the least movement without jostling others. Critics do not agree as to which side Balzac takes in this struggle between the individual and society. Certainly, after he joined the royalist party, he most often champions society in his formal statements. "Man is neither good nor bad," he wrote in the Preface to *La Comédie humaine,* "he is born with instincts and capacities; Society, far from depraving him, as Rousseau claimed, perfects him, makes him better." Throughout the *Comédie* Balzac refers to the danger of defying social law or custom. When Ginevra di Piombo marries without her father's consent, Balzac remarks: "At that point there began for her the apprenticeship of sorrow which society brings down upon those who reject its customs." His characters themselves, when they revolt, often admit their mistake. At the end of *Une Double Famille,* Granville exclaims: "Division between husband and wife, whatever the cause, brings terrible unhappiness: sooner or later we are punished for having disobeyed social law." Such passages, however, suggest no warmth of approval, but rather the admission of an inescapable fact. "Society practices none of the virtues it demands of men," Balzac wrote in *La Recherche de l'absolu;* "every hour it is committing crimes."

There is, on the other hand, a special sympathy for the free characters who struggle against society. We follow the careers of Eugène de Rastignac and Lucien de Rubempré with such eagerness because in their very ambition, selfish as it may be, we recognize Balzac's own creative drive. We may disapprove of Eugène, but we feel a kind of triumph in his success. We regret Lucien's failure; and if we are impatient with him, it is not so much for his antisocial qualities, as because his energy, his *volonté* are not strong enough. The great symbol of revolt is Vautrin, the criminal. Again and again Balzac presents him as diabolic. As he confronts Eugène, "His glance was that of the fallen archangel who still desires war"; but if he is fallen, he has the pride and strength of Lucifer. In his desire to mold destinies he is a creator. Even with Dr. Benassis and the Abbé Bonnet, it is perhaps not so much their goodness that impresses us as their power. Their humility is another and nobler kind of pride. They are not submitting to society, but of their own free will they are taking its part, imposing themselves upon it. The Abbé can sympathize with the passion of Véronique, which led to murder, because of its intensity, its integrity: "So the priest, overcome by the majesty of any great human feeling, even if it were criminal, judged of the greatness of this passion by the crime which it had caused."

What tempts Balzac's characters to pit their strength against society is the extraordinary energy they possess. Balzac was deeply interested in the theories of the Austrian mystic and physician Mesmer who, before his death in 1815, had won for himself a number of disciples in Paris. As a result of his experiments with hypnosis, Mesmer came to believe in a vital magnetic fluid, everywhere present in the universe, by means of which one human mind could directly influence or control another. Balzac often refers to this vital fluid, which he describes as "that *will* [*volonté*] so powerful between man and man, that nervous and fluid force, eminently mobile and transmissible." Every human being is born with a fixed amount of it. "A certain man is to another," he writes in the *Physiologie du mariage,* "as ten is to thirty, or one to five, and there is a degree which each of us cannot go beyond." Because of this fact, every man is faced with a problem, which Balzac describes symbolically in *La Peau de chagrin.* Raphaël Valentin receives from an antique dealer a piece of wild ass's skin which has the magic property of granting all of its owner's wishes; but as each wish comes true, the skin grows smaller, and its total disappearance means death. Raphaël reduces more and more his relations with the world, but no man can live quite without desire; at last—in spite of his agonized precautions —as the skin vanishes, he dies. Full living, then, means the expense of energy. If each man, even the genius, has a limited amount to spend, how careful should he be or how prodigal?

The struggle between action and contemplation, hoarding and spending, is one of the themes of *La Comédie humaine* because it haunted Balzac's own life. Part of the fear that seized him in the midst of his confidence and his triumph must have been a kind of vertigo caused by the tug of his creative energy, the sense of being rushed along toward an abyss; and when death came to him at the age of fifty with so much yet to be done, it was surely a result of his magnificent, his suicidal spending.

What concentrates this energy and sets it to work is passion; and here I am using the term very broadly—

74

including what Balzac calls "intérêt" and what he calls "amour"—to mean the intense, the overmastering craving to possess, to achieve, or to identify oneself with something. It may assume any form. Men ridden by a passion, as Vautrin says, "become infatuated with an idea and will not let go. They are thirsty only for a certain water from a certain spring; to drink of it they would sell their wives, their children, they would sell their souls to the devil."[33] Mischa Karamazov seems to echo Vautrin when he tells his brother Alyosha: "A man will fall in love with some beauty, with a woman's body, or even with a part of a woman's body (a sensualist can understand that) and he'll abandon his own children for her, sell his father and mother, and his country."

A passion may blind a man to everything but itself; but where it is concerned, it sharpens his wits, at once multiplies and concentrates his powers: "True passions have their instincts. Offer a gourmet a dish of fruit, he will make no mistake and even without looking he will help himself to the best piece." The passion may be social or political ambition, as with scores of characters; it may be vengeance, as with du Croisier and Cousine Bette; it may be a passion for women, as with Baron Hulot; it may be such a trifling thing as buying lottery tickets, as with Madame Descoings, or the possession of a certain room and its furnishings, as with Abbé Birotteau; it may be avarice in any number of forms—associated with the collector's love of art, with the craving for land, or most often with gold itself. One might say that the struggle for money is the common denomina-

[33] *Le Père Goriot,* VI, 268.

tor of various passions, for money is required to gratify most of them. Gold (or rather perhaps paper, the promises to pay, the notes that cannot be met, the shares with which Nucingen and du Tillet juggle) is also one of the main themes of *La Comédie humaine*.

Passion may take the form of disinterested devotion, like Eugénie Grandet's love for her cousin Charles or the adoration of Père Goriot for his daughters. Even avarice may be ennobled when, as in the case of Mlle de Pen-Hoël, it is practiced for the sake of others. It is a kind of moral passion that urges Dr. Benassis and the Abbé Bonnet to devote their lives to their communities. The intuition of the genius depends on his passionate self-identification with his art. But whether nobly or basely directed, passion, if not controlled, is dangerous,

Ayant l'expansion des choses infinies.

When the Lesbian, Madame de San-Réal, in her jealous rage has killed Paquita: "Adieu," she says to her brother de Marsay, who has been her rival, "nothing can console us for the loss of what has seemed infinite."[34] We think of Baudelaire and his *Femmes damnées*.

Beneath the passion in *La Comédie humaine* there is often a kind of suicidal impulse. In a passage that suggests both Dostoievski and Rimbaud, Balzac writes of the baneful power which the very idea of excess, of pushing any desire to its extreme limits may have over the imagination. He is writing of sensual debauch, but with a few verbal changes what he says might apply

[34] *La Fille aux yeux d'or*, XIII, 407.

to any of the passions—to avarice, to vengeance, even to creative genius:

Soon Debauchery appeared to me in all the majesty of its horror, and I understood it. Debauchery is certainly an art like poetry, and requires strength of soul. To grasp its mysteries, to taste its beauties a man must, in a certain fashion, devote himself to conscientious study. Like every field of knowledge, it is at first thorny and repulsive. Huge obstacles surround man's complete enjoyment, not his pleasures in detail but the systems which build up into a habit his rarest sensations, summarize them, enrich them for him by the creation of a dramatic other life within his life, by requiring an exorbitant, an immediate spending of his vital force.

All excesses are brothers. These social monstrosities exert the power of the abyss; they attract us as Saint Helena called Napoleon; they make our heads go round, they fascinate us and we want to peer into their depths without knowing why. Perhaps among these precipices there exists the idea of the infinite; perhaps they hide something that greatly flatters man.[35]

If passion unrestrained may lead even to murder, if in its last phases it may approach madness, there is underneath the surface of Balzac's world a kind of savagery that has not passion for its excuse. It is rather the survival of the animal in man—one of the signs that after all, in spite of his progress toward the light, he is not cut off by any sharp line from his brute beginnings. In the grey morning dusk after the banquet in *La Peau de chagrin,* the wan faces of the guests, "on which the physical appetites appeared stripped of the poetry with which the soul invests them, looked indescribably savage and coldly brutal." We are most

[35] *La Peau de chagrin,* XXVII, 172-73.

aware of this ferocity among the peasants, who would shoot at Dr. Benassis as he went on his rounds, or among the Chouans with their deliberate murder of Pille-Miche; but this is chiefly because then it appears without disguise. We may feel its hidden presence in the most sumptuous milieu, like an animal secretion used to give permanence or body to an expensive perfume.

In two of his stories Balzac actually breaks down the distinction between man and beast. Stéphanie, the heroine of *Adieu,* driven mad by the shock of her experiences in the retreat from Moscow, is reduced to an inhuman state. When Philippe, her former lover, offers her a lump of sugar at the suggestion of her attendant, she hesitates at first, like a wild beast torn between fear and desire. "At last the passion of the beast got the better of her fear; Stéphanie rushed to Philippe, snatched the sugar and disappeared into a clump of trees." We are given as it were the converse of this in *Une Passion dans le désert,* where Balzac, in a story discreetly filtered through two intermediate narrators, tells of the infatuation of a female panther for one of Napoleon's soldiers lost in the Egyptian desert.

8

Throughout *La Comédie humaine,* aerating it, as it were, like a dry breeze through the shadows of a forest, there moves a breath of real comedy, in the usual limited sense of the word; and I do not mean the occasional ponderous joke, or the conventional facetiousness that hides so much practical wisdom in the *Physiologie du mariage*. The real humor in the *Comédie* is quite different from this somewhat labored comic relief, just as it is different from the rowdy fun of the *Contes drolatiques*.[36]

It is a kind of irony reminiscent of Molière, a sense of the absurd, the incongruous in daily living. It sets the prevailing tone in *Le Député d'Arcis* with its picture of political intrigue, in *Pierre Grassou* with its sketch of the third-rate painter and his bourgeois clients, or in *Les Secrets de la princesse de Cadignan* where the experienced Diane convinces Daniel d'Arthez, the great writer, that she has always been the victim of malicious gossip. But we find it also in the most unexpected places—offsetting the emotional tension of *Béatrix,* sharpening the grimness of *Le Cousin Pons* and *La Cousine Bette*—so that the last novel is at the same time one of the most alarming and one of the most sardonically amusing things that Balzac ever wrote.

It is social satire, but it is rarely separated from individual characterization. When, for example, in *La Rabouilleuse* the scoundrel Philippe Bridau, to gain control of a fortune, insists that his moronic uncle marry the woman with whom he has lived for years, the local press brings out an edifying article: "All the friends of the church and the respectable people of our town witnessed yesterday a ceremony by which one of our most important property owners put an end to a

---

[36] Of course the *Contes drolatiques* contain many other elements than the earthy humor for which they are famous.

scandalous situation." It mentions the fact that the marriage was the result of Philippe's efforts and ends with the phrase: "Such disinterested behavior is rare enough to deserve the publicity we are giving it."[37] We may think of the passage as a satire on the press; yet its effect depends on our knowledge of the cynical Philippe.

César Birotteau explains to his wife that he hit upon the advertising campaign for his hair oil, Huile Céphalique, when he noticed that in a print of Hero and Leander, Hero was pouring oil upon her lover's head. His prospectus suggests the type of radio commercial with which we are all too familiar:

No lotion can make your hair grow, just as no chemical preparation can dye it without danger to the brain. Science has recently declared that hair is an inert substance and that no agent can keep it from falling or turning white. All you need to prevent xerasia and baldness is to protect the root bulbs from every external atmospheric influence and to keep your scalp at the proper temperature.[38]

And so it continues for several paragraphs of advertising copy which might serve as a model for an agency today. But all this is intimately connected with César himself: his delight, at once naive and shrewd, at finding the print and his inspiration in seeing what he could do with it; the clear conscience with which he, honest man that he is, makes use of such claptrap to lure the public.

Sometimes the social emphasis is less noticeable, and Balzac concentrates upon private idiosyncrasies, as in

[37] *La Rabouilleuse,* IX, 550.
[38] *César Birotteau,* XIV, 149.

the case of Mlle Cormon. The poor lady felt that in her *salons* it was her duty to talk, but she could never think of what to say; so she consulted her spiritual adviser.

This old priest, so strict in matters of discipline, had read to her a passage from Saint François de Sales about the duties of the *femme du monde,* and the decent gaiety of pious Christian women who should keep their severity for themselves and appear cheerful in their homes, so that their neighbors will not be bored.

After that Mlle Cormon would suffer tortures when conversation lagged and would be driven to make the most surprising statements. On one such occasion her remark, " 'Nobody but a little bird can be in two places at once,' successfully started a discussion on the ubiquity of the apostles, of which she could make nothing whatever." [39]

The satiric humor with which Balzac describes César Birotteau and Mlle Cormon is on the whole benign; the amusing description of the du Guénic family playing *mouche* in their old chateau at Guérande has the charm and warmth of Dickens when, for example, he introduces us to Wemmick's aged parent. More frequent, however, are touches of truly macabre comedy. If Madame Cibot, the brutal concierge, suggests in Balzac's own phrase a Lady Macbeth of the streets, she also suggests with her marvelous bursts of conversation the nurse in *Romeo and Juliet* and the terrible Sairey Gamp. The fact that she is not only cruel but amusing makes her only the more densely real and

[39] *La Vieille Fille,* X, 328-29.

therefore the more frightening. When the ex-perfumer Crevel tries to take advantage of Baron Hulot's infidelity to his wife, we are reminded of one of Fielding's more brutal episodes. There is the scene when the ambulance chaser Fraisier comes to tell the Présidente de Marville that her cousin Pons, whom she has treated cruelly, is dying and that he has a large estate which he intends to will out of the family unless Fraisier can prevent him.

"If that's the case," muttered the Présidente, astounded at the possible amount of the legacy, "I made a great mistake in quarreling with him, in attacking him."

"No, Madame [Fraisier replies reassuringly], for if you hadn't broken with him, he'd be as gay as a lark; he'd outlive you and Monsieur le Président and myself. Providence moves in its own ways. It's not for us to question them." [40]

9

We have seen that in *La Comédie humaine,* in spite of Balzac's secret sympathies, people suffer if they break social laws. There exists, however, a different kind of punishment, which Vautrin describes as follows: "There is in the course of events a power that you call *Providence,* that I used to call *chance.* Every evil action is caught up with, no matter how it tries to escape, by some vengeance or other." [41] At the end of *Ursule Mirouët,* after the brutal Minoret has been punished by the death of his son and Ursule finds

[40] *Le Cousin Pons,* XVIII, 229.
[41] *Splendeurs et misères,* XVI, 281.

the happiness she deserves, the Abbé Chaperon remarks: "The finger of God is in this." In *Le Cousin Pons*, when Rémonencq dies from swallowing the poison he had intended for his wife, Balzac comments: "Such an end, worthy of this scoundrel, points to the existence of Providence, which the chronicler of manners is accused of forgetting." There are other catastrophes which, though brought about by natural means, might suggest divine punishment.

The system of rewarding the good and punishing the bad is, of course, a cliché of the popular novel. As Oscar Wilde's Miss Prism remarks about her own lost manuscript: "The good ended happily, the bad unhappily. That is what Fiction means." If such punishments were the rule with Balzac, if we came to expect them as we do the intervention of the World Will to thwart Julian's plans in *Emperor and Galilean,* they would be a serious flaw in *La Comédie humaine*. They are, however, far from being the rule. Ursule is rewarded, but the equally deserving Eugénie Grandet and Adeline Hulot are not; the criminal Rémonencq is punished, but the worthy Pons and his unselfish friend Schmucke suffer more than he. One can never predict the fate of Balzac's characters.

What might be called the moral structure of *La Comédie humaine* has nothing to do with rewards and punishments. It is based, rather, on Balzac's contact (whether at first or second hand) with the writings of various mystics—the seventeenth-century German, Jacob Boehme, the eighteenth-century Frenchman, Saint-Martin, and most of all, Emanuel Swedenborg. As a very young man, Balzac read philosophy eagerly and unsystematically. Job, the hero of *Sténie,* writes to a friend:

I jump gaps too quickly. No sooner do I glimpse something than I see what it is driving at; no sooner is an argument presented than I see the outcome; I feel a principle, for me it is proved, while someone else is still wandering among the proofs; and I apply the principle, the argument, or the thing without being bothered by all these intermediate ideas.[42]

Balzac may well have been describing, with the complacency of youth, the impressionistic method with which he himself approached both philosophy and science.

Jacob Boehme's philosophy "attempts to harmonize the undeniable claim of Pantheism that God is not to be known out of and apart from nature, but in it and through it; with the equally undeniable fact of dualism, i.e. the evident opposition in this divine world of good and evil."[43] A similar attempt to reconcile the idea of essential unity with the problem of good and evil is to be found in both Swedenborg and Saint-Martin. Swedenborg "conceived of the universe as consisting of matter in different states of energy, and the 'soul' as being of the same energy substance as that element or state which is called 'magnetic.'"[44] For Saint-Martin, matter "is only a representation and an image of what is not material."[45] For each of these mystics, then, mat-

---

[42] *Sténie* (Paris, 1936), pp. 19-20.
[43] Paul Duessen in his Introduction to Jacob Boehme's *The Three Principles of the Divine Essence* (tr. John Sparrow; London, 1910), p. lii.
[44] Signe Toksvig, *Emanuel Swedenborg* (New Haven, 1948), p. 160.
[45] *Claude de Saint-Martin* in *Gnostiques de la Révolution* (ed. André Tanner; Paris, 1946), I, 89.

ter and spirit seem to be two aspects of one reality, aspects which intimately "correspond" to each other at every point; but for each man also there is a progression, a hierarchy, from the material to the immaterial, and all of them admit two realms or states, which they do not hesitate to call heaven and hell. They use such terms as "chain" or "ladder" to describe this progression. "Sensory objects and nature itself," writes Saint-Martin, "include only a part of that great ladder."[46] To Swedenborg, "the intercourse between the soul and the body is a kind of progression according to natural order by a ladder divided into degrees."[47] But "all the inhabitants of heaven and hell are derived from the human race."[48] Even on earth man can become, as it were, potentially an angel: "All that is here said of the angels and their turning to the Lord as a sun, is also to be understood of man as to his spirit, for man as to his mind is a spirit, and, if he be in love and wisdom, he is an angel."[49]

All of these ideas are referred to directly and indirectly in various parts of *La Comédie humaine*. In *Les Deux Rêves* the young Marat exclaims: "Nature became suddenly clear to me, and I grasped its immensity as I saw the ocean of beings who, scattered everywhere in groups and in species, were all parts of one sole and identical living substance, from the slab of marble to

---

[46] *Ibid.*, p. 103.
[47] Swedenborg. *The Economy of the Animal Kingdom,* as quoted in Toksvig, *Emanuel Swedenborg,* p. 109.
[48] Emanuel Swedenborg, *Heaven and Its Wonders, The World of Spirits, and Hell: From Things Heard and Seen* (New York, 1872), p. 156.
[49] Emanuel Swedenborg, *Angelic Wisdom concerning The Divine Love and Wisdom* (New York, 1875), p. 43.

God himself."[50] Sometimes, to support this idea, Balzac turned from mysticism to biology: "My first idea of *La Comédie humaine* was like a dream," he wrote in his famous Preface. "This idea came to me from a comparison between mankind and animals. There is only one animal. The creator made use of a single and identical pattern for all living organisms. The animal is a principle which assumes its outward form, or to speak more accurately, the differences in its form, from the environment in which it develops."[51]

But what gives the world of *La Comédie humaine* its special moral atmosphere is not Balzac's "philosophy" as he stated it formally. What we find in him is the illusion of experience itself and not a structure of original ideas about experience. Like so many of his age he was attracted to both philosophy and science, but he was neither a philosopher nor a scientist. He took his ideas, however, with the greatest seriousness; they served him as a kind of scaffolding to help him conceive and carry out his vast plan. The theories he accepted from philosophers, scientists, or even charlatans were a means of explaining to himself in abstract terms what he intimately and deeply felt. Once we have entered *La Comédie humaine,* we are aware of being plunged into a world that, however huge, is essentially one—not because Balzac tells us so, in phrases borrowed from Swedenborg or Saint-Martin, but because we perceive directly the relation of character to character and scene to scene. In the same way we are aware of a continual struggle between good and evil, a struggle

[50] *Les Deux Rêves*, XXX, 360.
[51] *Oeuvres complètes*, I, xxv-xxvi.

which often seems to involve powers greater and more mysterious than the consciences of the protagonists. We are also aware of a kind of hierarchy, a "ladder" of moral values depending on the spiritual nature of the characters. In the supernatural world which penetrates and surrounds the dense reality of *La Comédie humaine,* this ladder would ascend from the spirit of evil, incarnate in Balzac's Melmoth and Don Juan, to Séraphita-Séraphitus, the angel, who before the dazzled Minna and Wilfrid flies heavenward like the sun rising from the waves. On the purely human plane, the scale extends from what Balzac calls "the refuse of the human heart," as it appears in Fraisier or Marneffe or Philippe Bridau, to the saints and the geniuses.

Balzac was not, and knew he could never be, a saint. He was a genius, and it is perhaps in the treatment of genius that he is most self-revealing. Louis Lambert is a philosopher; Balthazar Claës is a chemist; Gambara is a musician; Frenhofer, a painter: each one loses contact with objective reality. We feel that Claës is doomed from the start: he is seeking the "Absolute"— the common basis of all matter—although the Absolute, as a symbol, has also its more usual meaning. Louis Lambert, in his quest for absolute knowledge or truth, is lost in his own remote world from which he cannot return to the world of men. Frenhofer, in his struggle to paint a perfect picture, has worked secretly for years; and when at last he displays it, it is unintelligible even to his brother artists. Gambara, who improvises divinely when he is drunk, has composed an opera which no one can listen to. "My music is beautiful," he explains, "but when music goes beyond sensation to become idea, its hearers must be men of genius, for they alone have the power to develop it." Of Frenhofer, Balzac asks: "Was he rational or mad? Was he the slave of an artist's whim, or were the ideas he had expressed the result of that indescribable fanaticism produced in us by the long gestation of a great work?"[52]

Through these four men Balzac presents the mystery of genius, with its quest for what always just escapes—the unattainable "absolute" of its vision. This quest filled Balzac with ecstasy as something divine, but it also filled him with terror as a profanation, like the crime of Prometheus—a path that might lead to madness. But the border line between madness and genius, between the lost and the saved, may not be so sharp as it appears. That, I think, is what he is suggesting in the tragedies of Frenhofer and Gambara. The usual interpretation of their stories is that they are portraits of two men whose insistence on perfection, whose refusal to recognize the limits set to everything human have made them intellectualize their art to such an extent that it has passed beyond the borders of art to become a kind of private gibberish. Frenhofer's mistake was to neglect the principle stated by his friend Porbus: "Painters should meditate only with brush in hand." Gambara's was to try to make music pass beyond sensation to the pure expression of ideas.

This is one meaning of the stories; but it seems to me that they contain also another meaning—a kind of half-hidden irony at the expense not of the artists but of their baffled and pitying spectators. Significantly, Boehme writes: "Therefore should I speak and write

[52] *Le Chef-d'oeuvre inconnu,* XXVIII, 27.

that which is purely heavenly, and altogether of the clear Deity, I should be as dumb to the reader, who hath not the knowledge and the gift."[53] In Swedenborg's hierarchy, "The wisdom of the angels of the third or inmost heaven is incomprehensible even to the inhabitants of the ultimate [outer] heaven."[54] This is how Gambara explains his own predicament: "My trouble came from listening to the concerts of the angels and thinking that men could understand them." Is it not possible that Frenhofer's picture, that Gambara's opera were in reality works of such heavenly genius that they were beyond the reach of ordinary mortals? I do not think that one interpretation precludes the other; in fact, the coexistence of the two meanings comes close to being the expression of what is most central, what is deepest in Balzac's nature—with its joy of life and its despair, its craving for order and for rebellion, its tendency to see in everything human the two sides of the medal.

Sometimes when we are driving on a rainy night along a city street, the lamps at the corners, the lights of approaching cars, the reflections on the wet asphalt may suddenly become a two-dimensional pattern. For a dazed moment the eye can no longer interpret them as real objects seen in perspective: there is no street; there are no cars; we might be looking through a gigantic telescope at the spots and streaks in some star cluster in the darkness of outer space. So may a work of genius appear to its contemporaries until they have learned to interpret its signs, to feel the life, the

[53] Boehme, *The Three Principles of the Divine Essence*, p. 11.
[54] Swedenborg, *Heaven and Hell*, p. 128.

order beneath what may at first seem arbitrary or mad distortion. But conversely, the genius himself, with his ability to enter the minds of others, may perhaps catch himself looking at his own work from their point of view; the street, the lights, the ordered vision may dissolve into a blur of spots and dashes. What if, after all, the crowd is right? What if there is nothing there? It is such dreadful moments, it seems to me, that Balzac is suggesting in *Gambara* and *Le Chef-d'oeuvre inconnu*.

Perhaps it was this doubt of Frenhofer's and Gambara's, even more than Raphaël's fear of death as he watched the magic skin, that explains Balzac's moments of despair. His fight was not so much against the surrounding world, against the mediocrity that is always, with a terrifying lack of malice, encroaching upon and denying the first rate. The real battle was in his own mind. As the saint must sometimes have to struggle to keep his faith in God, so the true struggle of the genius must be to keep his faith in himself—the struggle against damnation and against madness. Something of the magnitude of that tragic conflict is reflected in the struggles of Balzac's characters, to add dignity and intensity to the world of *La Comédie humaine*. This may have been partly what Baudelaire had in mind when he said that all of Balzac's characters had genius.

Balzac has been critcized for ridiculing, or failing to understand ordinary human goodness. In his famous essay, Taine writes: "Balzac counts the stammerings, the warts, the bad habits, all the small inanities, all the ugly things that we meet in the virtuous man as in other men," and for Taine this is a diminishing of

90

virtue. Le Breton, echoing him, goes even further: "When [Balzac] wants to describe virtue, he instinctively makes it appear ugly or ridiculous." Both men seem to suggest that true virtue depends on attractive externals, that it cannot survive the absurd. Balzac does not ridicule virtue: he merely shows that it needs no help from cosmetics. The stupid utterly bourgeois César Birotteau may, when tested, show a delicate sense of honor, just as the slovenly and naive Schmucke may show the most admirable devotion. Alain, with a touch of paradox, suggests that Balzac describes virtue so convincingly because he is indifferent to it. I should say rather that he is content to let it shine by its own light.

But just as important as this kind of spiritual scale in determining the moral effect of *La Comédie humaine* is something that Balzac never tried to express in abstract terms because it was too intimately a part of himself for him to be able to see it or judge it. Baudelaire, who understood him so well, suggested it when, with Balzac specifically in mind, he made this statement about certain writers of genius: "However great may be the sorrows that overtake them, however discouraging the human spectacle, their healthy temperaments always in the end prevail, and perhaps something better, which is a deep natural wisdom."[55]

[55] Charles Baudelaire, *Oeuvres complètes* (Paris, 1951), p. 960.

PART III

The Characters

So we are always forced to explain the mysteries
of the mind by material comparisons.

—*La Peau de chagrin*

1

The energy and passion with which Balzac's world is charged, the ironic comedy that flashes across it are of course expressed through the natures of its inhabitants. Any aspect of Balzac leads without a break into every other. His picture of Paris may be thought of as a kind of group portrait of the Parisian, just as his pictures of rooms and houses help define the individuals who live in them. But Balzac's characters emerge from the shadows of their surrounding world to exist solidly and intensely in their own right.

E. M. Forster in his *Aspects of the Novel* states that the difference between fictional characters and real people lies in the fact that the characters of the novelists, unlike ourselves, live in a world where their secret life is visible, and adds that their reality depends on the novelist's knowing everything about them, even if he may keep some of it hidden. "He will give us the feeling that though the character has not been explained, it is explicable." It does not seem to me, however, that this is quite the case. I should say that the great novelist knows so much about his characters, has given them such a fullness of life, that he is aware he does not and cannot know everything. Forster's statement might suggest that the novelist had in his possession a number of neatly labeled cards about, say, Prince Myshkin, or Fabrice del Dongo, or Véronique Sauviat. There might be many or few, but there would always be a definite and limited number. One might have a 500-

card character and show only 350 cards, or a 20-card character and show only 15; but however great the number, once the cards were all read the character would be *completely* explained and presented: of Myshkin or Fabrice or Véronique there would be, even as a possibility, *nothing more*.

With Balzac or Dostoievski or Proust, there is always the suggestion of possible change, of something more which even the writer has not caught: it is Balzac's very sense of his character's reality that prevents a complete enumeration, just as it was Pascal's lucidity that convinced him of the bounds of reason. In fact, I should say it is this element of indeterminacy that distinguishes many of the characters of the greatest novelists from those of the lesser great. The regions of Trollope and Zola, for example, are spacious and solid, and certainly filled with life; but what for the most part they lack is depth and mystery: such novelists *do* know everything that is to be known about their characters; they can imagine nothing that eludes them, and that is why, in spite of the vigor of their talent, we may feel in them a limitation.

But there are two ways of not knowing a character. The minor novelist may fail to see him as an entity, an organic being, so that the character is either prodded along some predetermined logical course or made to perform arbitrarily *un acte gratuit*. With the great novelist there is no such fumbling. The character is there: he does exist with his own life, and certainly the writer knows more about him than any of his readers can know; but he exists as a whole; he possesses an intimate personal substance, like the arrangement of cells

96

in a living organism. His creator can no more "explain" him than Mozart could explain one of his own themes, or Renoir the life in his radiant young women.

2

Among the two thousand characters who people *La Comédie humaine* there are many who are presented largely as typical; and there is perhaps no single character, however individualized, who may not be seen (before we come to know him well) as typifying something or other. The characters in the *Etudes de moeurs,* Balzac wrote Madame Hanska, are *des individualités typisées;* those in the *Etudes philosophiques* are *des types individualisées.* There are the social types—such as César Birotteau, the Restoration bourgeois in commerce, or Gaudissart, the traveling salesman, or the Duchesse de Langeais, the lady of the Faubourg Saint-Germain—into each of whose portraits Balzac was able to pour much of his observation of many different people belonging to a particular group, and thus through the individual to illumine the group as a whole. There are also the "philosophic" types—such as Raphaël Valentin or Balthazar Claës—who seem to represent an idea, or at least a very general human attitude: with Raphaël the struggle between contemplation and action, with Balthazar "the quest of the Absolute." One might add a third group which would share certain qualities of each of the two I have mentioned: namely, such characters as Père Grandet, representing avarice;

Baron Hulot, sexual obsession; or Théodose de La Peyrade, hypocrisy. One might class these, at least in inception, as "moral" types after the tradition of Molière: they represent not so much historico-social groups (like Birotteau) or abstract ideas (like Raphaël), as permanent human traits.

But as we scrutinize the characters in any of these groups, we see that the division is, after all, superficial. If the Duchesse de Langeais is a social type, one might think of her also, like Valentin, as representing the struggle between emotional hoarding and spending, or, like Célimène, as representing eternal feminine coquetry. César Birotteau might be not only the prosperous shopkeeper of the Restoration, but human naiveté or perhaps good-natured honesty. Again he might be thought of as an illustration of the idea that pride goeth before a fall.

When faced with such a crowd of characters as we meet in *La Comédie humaine,* it is easy to picture them, as Alain expresses it, in "series": there are the young girls, the men about town, the journalists, the misers. Members of any series may strike us as typical or they may not. None of the series is like a company of soldiers lined up at an equal distance from the spectator: some members may be so far away that we can make out hardly more than the color of their uniforms; with the nearest, we forget their uniforms, because their faces have all the detailed sharpness of Rembrandt portraits.

We have only a passing glimpse of many of these characters, and naturally they impress us in terms of one or two surface traits, like the friend of one of our friends whom we have met at a public reception or a dinner party. Take, among innumerable examples, Maître Massol, whom Balzac presents to us virtually in a single phrase as "one of those lawyers who assume that eloquence is the faculty of talking indefinitely, who possess the secret of boring no matter what they say, the curse of meetings where they reduce everything to the most petty level, and who must make themselves important at any price."[1] At home he may be a tyrant or an ideal family man; in an emergency he might be a coward or a hero. We could place him near the end of the series of lawyers, headed by Maître Derville or Monsieur de Granville.

Seen in more detail than Massol, but still a background character, who might be placed in a series of provincial notables, is Monsieur de Saintot, president of the Agricultural Society of Angoulême.

Astolphe had the reputation of being a first-rate scholar. Ignorant as a carp, he had none the less written the articles on *sugar* and *brandy* for an Agricultural Dictionary, by lifting details from all the newspaper articles and previous books that dealt with these products. The whole Department thought he was at work on a treatise on modern farming. Although he would lock himself up all morning in his study, he had not written two pages in a dozen years. If anyone came to see him, he would be discovered shuffling papers, looking for a mislaid note or sharpening his pen; but the whole time he spent in his room was wasted on trifles: he would read through the local newspaper or carve corks with his penknife or make doodles on his blotting-pad; he would thumb the leaves of his Cicero in the hope his eye might fall on a sentence or a passage which might be applied to current events; then that evening he would drag into the conversa-

[1] *Une Fille d'Eve,* IV, 154.

tion some topic which would give him the chance to remark:
"There's a page in Cicero which might have been written
about what's happening today." Then he would recite his
passage to the amazement of his hearers who would repeat
among themselves: "Really, there's nothing Astolphe doesn't
know!"[2]

The paragraph suggests one of La Bruyère's
Caractères. Various personal pecularities are mentioned; we see Astolphe as we might see a man whom
we meet only on rare occasions though we have known
him for years. Balzac shows him in two lights whose
contrast results in an effect of irony: as he appears to
his little group, and as he "really" is (i.e., as he appears
to his creator). His function in the story is to give a
sense of the local society that Lucien de Rubempré
meets at Madame de Bargeton's. Astolphe is himself an
example of that society and helps define the group as
a whole by the impression he makes upon it. Like a
minor dancer in a ballet, he is given only one chance
to perform a solo figure; but afterwards, as we see
him among the others, we recognize him in passing.
We know that he, like all the rest of them who have
also had their moments, could if the ensemble required
it do a great deal more than his subordinate rôle per-
mits.

I might give one other example of a typed character,
treated with still greater fullness than Monsieur de
Saintot: the Vicomtesse de Kergarouet who appears
for a scene in *Béatrix*. As with Massol and Astolphe,
Balzac paints for us a sharp "portrait," this time in

[2] *Illusions perdues*, XI, 258-59.

100

a single long sentence; but here he allows the personage to illustrate by her own talk some of the points he has made in introducing her.

As for the Vicomtesse de Kergarouet, she was typically provincial: tall, dry, faded, with secret pretentions which only appeared when her feelings had been hurt; an incessant talker who had won a reputation for wit by now and then striking an idea, as a billiard player makes a point by hitting one ball with another; eager to put Parisians in their place with the alleged shrewdness and good nature of the provinces and the flaunting of an assumed contentment; stooping in the hope of being asked to rise and furious at being left on her knees; dressing sloppily and yet in extreme styles; mistaking bad manners for aristocratic insolence and imagining she could worry people with her snubs; refusing what she wanted, to induce a second offer and appear to be extravagantly urged; interested in obsolete topics and amazed at being behind the times; finally just waiting to drag in Nantes, the social lights of Nantes, the fashionable affairs of Nantes, complaining of Nantes, criticizing Nantes, and taking as a personal insult the absent-minded acquiescence of those who politely agreed with her.[3]

When we first meet her, she has arrived with her daughter Charlotte for a visit to Guérande. The famous woman novelist Camille Maupin, who has just been presented to them, offers them a lift in her carriage. Madame de Kergarouet apologizes for not having come in her own; but, after all, traveling in that way is expensive and her visit must be short because "three other little kittens" are impatiently waiting for her at home. It occurs to her that it would be a gracious gesture to ask Camille how she writes her books.

[3] *Béatrix,* V, 155.

"Just as you do your sewing," Camille replies, "your crocheting, or your cross-stitch."

"But how do you ever think up all your deep remarks and your lovely descriptions?"

"The way you think up the amusing things you say, Madame. There's nothing so easy as writing, and if you wanted to . . ."

"You mean that any one can write if he really wants to? I shouldn't have thought so. And which of your books is your favorite?"

"It's hard to choose among one's own little kittens."

"Of course you must be blasé on compliments. One can't think up anything new to say."

"Believe me, Madame, I appreciate the form of yours."[4]

We are shown little more of the Vicomtesse. She is not introduced, like Monsieur de Saintot, merely to give life to a circle whose group action affects the leading characters: she plays in a small way her own individual part in the drama; but she too remains, as Balzac labels her, "a provincial type."

There are in *La Comédie humaine* hundreds of such transitory characters; and just as we are shown more of Madame de Kergarouet than of Monsieur Massol, so we see more of others than we do of Madame de Kergarouet. In fact there is nowhere a fixed line between the major and minor characters. Even among the most lightly sketched, however, it is hard to find two exactly alike; and Balzac shows them, as he does his houses and landscapes, not merely as they may appear but as they exist in themselves, though the degree of penetration and the level at which we see them vary.

[4] *Ibid.*, p. 160.

Not even Camille Maupin, during their short meeting, could discover all that Balzac tells us about Madame de Kergarouet.

We meet references—complimentary or not—to the eccentricity of Balzac's minor characters, as if he had gone out of his way to collect a quaint and unusual group of "extras." Nothing, it seems to me, could be further from the truth. Most of those we meet, like Maître Massol or Monsieur de Saintot or Madame de Kergarouet, are not in themselves unusual. What is unusual is the sharpness with which Balzac sees them, the way he presents them to us in a few strokes. If most people seem without color to most of us, it is because of our own dim eyesight. No one, however swiftly seen, was colorless to Balzac any more than to Daumier.

3

In his little book, *Le Roman,* François Mauriac makes the statement: "A hero of Balzac's is always coherent. There is not one of his actions that cannot be explained by his dominant passion."[5] The tendency to write of Balzac's characters as if they were all of a piece, each one "built around" some inflexible trait, has perhaps been emphasized by the recent fashion of regarding human nature as itself incoherent and unpredictable. Mauriac goes on to say:

[5] François Mauriac, *Le Roman* (Paris, 1928), pp. 47–48. In his Preface to Claude Mauriac's book, *Aimer Balzac* (Paris, 1945), his attitude is much more understanding.

Let's look about us, let's choose someone at random and try to judge him definitively, without any preconceived idea. Inevitably we shall run into a thousand contradictions and the chances are that in the end we shall make no pronouncement. If, on the other hand, we examine a hero or heroine of the Balzacian type of novel, it will not take us long to apply the label "sympathetic" or "antipathetic," if not "infamous" or "sublime."[6]

Mauriac seems to be making two interrelated statements: that as we look at people, it becomes more and more difficult to decide what "kind of people" they are, and hence more and more difficult to pronounce moral judgments upon them. As to the formulating of definitive moral judgments, I should agree that it is never easy; but this is something that Balzac rarely does. When it comes to determining people's "kinds," however, the difficulty would seem to depend upon which of our acquaintances we choose to observe. If one of our neighbors becomes more and more puzzling, another perhaps will seem more and and more consistent. No matter how much, as scientists or as artists, we may think of people's personalities as a succession of loosely related "attitudes" or "rôles," we still practically consider them as entities. Our wives and children, our friends and colleagues, our enemies and tormentors remain for us "themselves," even if we deny that the word "self" has valid meaning.

This is also true of most of the people in first-rate novels. As we read Virginia Woolf, her characters may seem to melt away into the quiet iridescence of par-

[6] Mauriac, *Le Roman,* p. 50.

ticular moments; as we read Proust, his characters—themselves always in flux—may appear the more elusive because the mirror that reflects them is never still. But as we remember them, Mrs. Dalloway and Mrs. Ramsay, at least, seem "real people" in much the way that Elizabeth Bennet and Fanny Price seem real: we could imagine them talking to each other across a gulf of time. The Baron de Charlus becomes as much a coherent entity as Sam Weller, though one hopes for both their sakes that they may never meet in the Elysian fields. Of course human behavior may be unpredictable, it may seem self-contradictory; but also it may fall into relatively consecutive and predictable patterns. As Gertrude Stein remarks: "All men and all women, if they keep on in their living come to the repeating that makes it clear to any one who listens to them then the real nature of them."[7]

If the behavior of most people is not so incoherent as we might gather from the remarks of some recent critics, Balzac's characters, on the other hand, are not nearly so rigid as many of his readers have assumed. Certainly they develop; they do often surprise; even the "monomanes" are given qualities unrelated, at least in the beginning, to their obsessions. This seems so obvious when we read the novels themselves that it is hard to account for the conventional attitude. Before taking up the major figures, I shall give an example of one of the hundreds of minor characters, unpredictably developed, who crowd what might be called the middle distance of *La Comédie humaine*.

[7] Gertrude Stein, *The Making of Americans, Being a History of a Family's Progress* (Paris, n.d.), p. 141.

Monsieur de Bargeton is the husband of one of the heroines of *Illusions perdues:*

This gentleman had one of those small minds, placidly poised between the harmless insignificance that still can grasp what is said and the intrepid dullness that refuses to accept or exchange the slightest idea. Impressed by his duties toward society, he struggled to make himself agreeable and had reduced his means of expression to the fixed smile of the ballet. Pleased or displeased, he would still smile. He would smile at news of some disaster or of the most auspicious event. This smile of his could be adjusted to serve any purpose. If he was absolutely forced to express downright approval, he underlined it with a compliant laugh, but did not utter a word if he could help it. A tête-à-tête was the only real complication that disturbed his vegetative existence: he had then to fish for some remark in the immensity of his inner void. Usually he escaped by reverting to the artless habits of his childhood: he would think aloud; he would confide in you the most trivial details of his life; he would tell you of his petty needs and feelings which, for him, took the place of ideas. He did not talk about the weather or indulge in the usual bromides which protect the feeble-minded: he would turn instead to the most intimate personal details.

"I ate some veal this morning, to please Madame de Bargeton. She's very fond of it, but it seems to have upset me. I knew it would. It always does. I've no idea why." Or: "I'm going to ring for a glass of sugar and water. Wouldn't you like one too?" Or: "I'm going riding tomorrow. I shall call on my father-in-law."

Since these remarks offered little chance for discussion, beyond a *yes* or a *no,* the conversation would collapse.[8]

If we were to see no more of Monsieur de Bargeton, we should think of him solely in terms of his idio-

[8] *Illusions perdues,* XI, 250-51.

syncrasy; he would suggest one of Henri de Régnier's provincial silhouettes in *Les Vacances d'un jeune homme sage.* The reader may recall Mlle Cormon, who was also tormented by having to find things to say to her guests. In each case Balzac is describing the same trait; in each case it becomes a living part of the character and in so doing is at once differentiated. As Balzac remarks in *La Vieille Fille,* "It is absurd to reduce feelings to identical formulae; as they occur in each man they fuse with elements peculiar to himself and assume his individual expression."

In the case of Monsieur de Bargeton, Balzac goes on to speak of his relations to his wife:

Anaïs was the joy of his life; she made him infinitely happy. When she played her role as hostess, he would relax in an easy chair to admire her, for she would assume his share in the conversation: then it had become one of his pleasures to try to catch the point of her remarks, and as often he could not discover it until long after she had made them, his smiles were like the delayed explosions of cannon balls buried in the ground. Anaïs, with her cleverness and generosity, had not taken advantage of her husband in recognizing his childlike nature, which gratefully accepted her domination. She had taken care of him as you might take care of a cloak; she kept him neat and brushed, protected him, humored him; and Monsieur de Bargeton, feeling himself humored, brushed and cared for, had come to feel a dog-like devotion to his wife.[9]

From the first part of the portrait we could not have predicted the second: we might have thought rather that Monsieur de Bargeton was indifferent to his wife,

[9] *Ibid.,* pp. 251-52.

afraid of her, or incapable of strong feeling; and although by this time we have seen a great deal of Madame de Bargeton, we should have imagined she would treat her husband with mild contempt or impatient irony. The few lines telling of their relationship add something to both their characters, and in so doing cause a slight shift in our judgment of all the traits we thought we knew.

But the final revelation of Monsieur de Bargeton's nature is yet to come. One morning Lucien de Rubempré is discovered on his knees before Madame de Bargeton by Stanislas de Chandour, an elderly local dandy, who cannot resist spreading the news through the *salons* of Angoulême. Madame de Bargeton at once gives her husband her own version of the episode, innocent enough in itself, and tells him that he should challenge Stanislas to a duel. As a matter of course, Monsieur de Bargeton sets out to obey her request.

"People who live like Monsieur de Bargeton," Balzac then tells us, "in a silence imposed by the limited range of their intelligence, possess, for the major circumstances of life, a ready-made solemnity." Monsieur de Bargeton finds Stanislas at home among a number of guests. He calls him aside and when Chandour, considering him merely an absurd elderly man, repeats that he found Madame de Bargeton and Lucien in a compromising situation, Monsieur de Bargeton replies:

All right. If you don't take back your remark in front of the present company, I must ask you to find a second. My father-in-law, Monsieur de Nègrepelisse, will call for you at four o'clock in the morning. Let's each make our arrangements, for the affair can only be settled as I've suggested. I choose pistols, since I'm the offended party.[10]

Stanislas, amazed, is terrified to accept but ashamed to withdraw; the duel is fought. Monsieur de Bargeton fires the first shot and wounds him in the neck, Stanislas falls to the ground, and the duel is over.

When Lucien, informed of the duel by a note from Madame de Bargeton, calls on her later in the day: "He found Naïs lunching with her husband who, hungry after his morning's jaunt, was eating with no concern for what had happened."

That is virtually all we see of Monsieur de Bargeton, but he has become a three-dimensional character. His behavior, if you like, is "logical," in the sense that *after* it has occurred it convinces you; but on the surface it is most surprising. Nothing would seem farther from his usual dependence and social ineptitude than the dignity and matter-of-fact courage with which he met a situation that might have been humiliating. This revelation is the result of a necessary episode in the plot: Balzac had to imagine some event to explain Madame de Bargeton's leaving Angoulême for Paris. No one can say whether he first thought of the duel and then realized what Monsieur de Bargeton's rôle would be; or whether, considering Monsieur de Bargeton, he saw that he was just the man to show his real quality in a duel and so invented the incident.

[10] *Ibid.*, pp. 321-22.

4

As we watch the development of a character, we may become aware that two different things are taking place. There is our own gradual or swift discovery of traits that were already there but whose presence we had not suspected. Our idea of the character changes, but that is not the result of any change in him: it comes from the widening of our knowledge, the deepening of our perception. By the time we meet Monsieur de Bargeton he has no doubt reached the stage where his life is a continuous repeating. Although the duel surprised us, he was the same man after he fought it as he was before.

There are people, on the other hand, both in books and in life, who seem actually themselves to change as we watch them, to become in certain ways different people from the ones we had formerly known. Of course it would be impossible to say just when a shift in emphasis or arrangement of attitudes already there becomes under stress of experience actual "change" in personality, just as it is sometimes hard for our courts to draw a line between normal behavior and insanity. There are people, however, who at one time held responsible positions in society and later have become patients in mental hospitals: between the two stages a change of some sort has occurred.

It is, as one would expect, in the characters presented at greatest length that we are apt to find this second type of change, and also it is in those whom we first meet in their youth. Eugène de Rastignac and Lucien de Rubempré, when they come to Paris, are naive young men full of good intentions; each one is corrupted by the struggle for success. Eugène adapts himself to his world at the cost of most of his scruples; Lucien, through a kind of softness and lack of self-knowledge, is driven to suicide. Even those obsessed by the idea that Balzac's personalities are, from the start, "fixed" often grant that Lucien and Eugène are exceptions. For this reason, I have chosen another character to illustrate the free way in which many of Balzac's protagonists do change and develop—Dinah de La Baudraye, the heroine of *La Muse du département*.

We are introduced to Dinah as a provincial bluestocking, one of the women who, throughout France in the 1830's, were led astray by the influence of George Sand and considered themselves writers of talent and passion. She might be treated as another provincial type in the manner of La Bruyère, a kind of pendant to Madame de Kergarouet. After a few scenes, however, we are taken into her past, and she begins to develop.

Descended from a well-to-do protestant bourgeois family, she abjures Calvinism at seventeen in the hope of finding an aristocratic husband and succeeds in marrying Monsieur de La Baudraye, a tiny wizened man more than twice her age. Her beauty, helped by the suspicion that her marriage is platonic, attracts a group of men around her. "As she noticed her ecstatic listeners, she gradually formed the habit of listening to herself; she began to love talking for its own sake and to look at her friends as so many confidants in a classical tragedy, whose function it was merely to give her her

111

cues."[11] Meanwhile she tries and fails to understand her husband; she becomes enthusiastic about the romantic movement, and even writes under a pseudonym a long romantic poem, *Paquita la Sévillane.* "In six years Dinah reflected the tone of her society. Since she saw only men, she had, without realizing it, assumed a mannish air; she thought she could escape their absurdities by making fun of them; but as sometimes happens, certain tints of what she ridiculed had colored her own nature."[12]

At this point Etienne Lousteau, a literary hack and journalist, comes to Sancerre from Paris on a political errand. Tired out by sixteen years of rather dingy struggle, bald and aged at thirty-seven, he can none the less still be charming to women. Dinah invites him to stay at her house and sets out at once, in a manner that recalls the villa of Madame de Cambremer, to dazzle him by her comments on the narrowness of provincial life. Lousteau remarks to one of her admirers that he considers her more loquacious than witty. The remark comes back to her.

This noble Dinah who would not give herself to fools, who, in the depths of her province led a terrible existence of struggles, of repressed revolt, of unpublished poems and who, to escape Lousteau, had just climbed the loftiest and steepest pinnacle of her disdain, who would not have come down if she had seen this pseudo-Byron begging for mercy at her feet, suddenly toppled from her height as she thought of her album. Madame de La Baudraye had the mania for collecting autographs.[13]

[11] *La Muse du département,* X, 71.
[12] *Ibid.,* p. 86.
[13] *Ibid.,* p. 106.

She cannot bear to see Lousteau leave the house without writing his name and some appropriate sentiment in her book.

Lousteau's vanity is aroused by the tales he hears of her unapproachability, and before long, for the first time, she falls deeply, ardently in love. "Dinah was alive! She had found a use for her energy; she discovered unexpected prospects in her future; she was happy at last." When Lousteau returns to Paris, he forgets the affair; but some time later she appears in his rooms, announcing that she is pregnant. Soon he is caught by a passion almost as genuine as hers. "In that perfect intimacy where each one puts aside his mask, the young woman kept her modesty, let him see the virile integrity and drive, peculiar to ambitious people, which was the foundation of her character. So in spite of himself Lousteau came to respect her."[14]

When her son is born, household expenses increase. Lousteau, a man of no continuity either in his work or in his emotions, begins to tire of her. Seeing this,

Dinah wanted to be necessary; she wanted to give something of her energy to this man whose weakness smiled upon her, because she saw in it a guarantee for herself. She found him subjects; she planned his books for him; if necessary she wrote entire chapters; she put new blood into the veins of his exhausted talent; she offered him her ideas and her criticisms.[15]

A second child discourages Lousteau completely. Dinah knows that he has returned to his former promiscuous

14 *Ibid.*, p. 206.
15 *Ibid.*, p. 221.

ways, and to keep any self-respect she decides to make her relation to him a purely maternal one; yet sometimes even so, when to extract money from her he returns to his old caresses, she cannot resist her passion,

finding in it the sharpest pleasure, the delights of the damned. When this woman with such a virile mind thought of being left alone, she felt her courage give way. She preferred the foreseen inevitable tortures of this savage intimacy to the loss of delights all the more exquisite for being born in remorse, in terrible struggles with herself: the eternal *no* that would end by being changed into *yes*.[16]

Six years after Dinah's flight to Paris, Monsieur de La Baudraye becomes count and peer of France. Quite cynical in regard to his wife's affair, he would like her now to keep house for him, as a beautiful and distinguished hostess, and wants to accept her two sons as his own. Again her destiny is influenced by a chance trifle. She meets a school friend who has previously cut her at the theatre, and once more Dinah is ignored. "I am a countess," she says to herself. "I shall have a salon, with the leading lights of politics and literature, and then *I* will look at *her*."

One evening when Lousteau comes home, he finds her dressed and ready to go out. "Your cook's giving notice, my dear," she tells him. "Madame de La Baudraye is taking you to dinner at the Rocher de Cancale."

In spite of his pleading, now that he is made to realize how much he depends on her, she leaves him to act as hostess in Monsieur de La Baudraye's Paris residence. She collects about her a respectable social circle

[16] *Ibid.,* p. 232.

114

and takes a day at home. "Dinah conquered in Paris by her silence as she conquered in Sancerre by her talk. An occasional epigram, or a comment when someone had made a fool of himself, showed her to be a woman quite at home with ideas."[17]

But even now Dinah is not happy. After some months Lousteau calls on her to beg for money. She feels sorry for him and arranges to let him have six thousand francs. Their eyes meet. Passion flares up once more. She hides him as her mother comes into the room and at once sends her on an errand.

Ten days later Dinah and her children, with a tutor, return to Sancerre for the summer. "She was charming, everyone said, with the Count."

That is where we leave her. At no time in her career could we have predicted what she would do or what she would feel. Though Balzac refers to the strength of the ambitious person as being the basis of her character, she is always doing things that work against her ambition; again and again she gives way to weakness. Her life for a time is dominated by Lousteau, and yet she leaves him quite suddenly—only to return to him on one chance occasion months after their break. The quality of her passion changes during its course from a proud and romantic devotion to a guilt-obsessed physical bondage. Several times in her life major actions are determined by what one would have thought of as irrelevant trifles. The artless garrulous Muse who ruled over the society of Sancerre and sent romantic verse to the local papers could not even have imagined the sophisticated embittered woman who, when she

[17] *Ibid.*, p. 244.

broke with Lousteau, invited him to dine with her at the Rocher de Cancale.

In trying to give an impression of Dinah, I have inevitably simplified and distorted because her uniqueness is the result of innumerable touches. We cannot really catch the effect of her changing unless we see with equal sharpness the character of Lousteau. He is doomed to repeat, and as we read of him we learn the nature of his repeating; but it is not until we have nearly finished the book that we realize that he himself recognizes, with a mixture of cynicism and desperation, his own inescapable doom. The relation between Dinah and her lover might suggest a constantly progressing and unfolding melody above a recurrent base.

5

The more closely we scrutinize Balzac's characters, the more we see that he uses the same manner of approach to nearly all of them. It is because of this particular approach, which may be described both as a technical method of treating character and the special way in which Balzac perceives it, that he is able to give us such variety, that his people appear at once so sharply defined and so undefinable.

One can never know from where a great novelist received the first idea, the germ, of any of the people he has created. Often, no doubt, he is not himself quite sure, and it is naive to accept too literally his own explanations. In a letter to Madame Hanska Balzac writes: "I have never *made a portrait* of anyone, except G. Planche in Claude Vignon, with his permission, and G. Sand, in Camille Maupin, likewise with her permission." Later he tells her: "Dablin, the old retired hardware dealer, my first friend, is the original of César Birotteau," and in his letter to Hyppolite Castille he assures him that the model for Vautrin exists. The statements are not contradictory: one may take suggestions from a living person without portraying him. Many people (including Balzac himself) have been identified, more or less plausibly, as the originals of characters in *La Comédie humaine*.

Most often, it would seem to me, their origins are a mixture of what might seem incongruous elements. The anonymous model for Vautrin to whom Balzac alludes was most probably Vidocq; yet Vautrin stems from the hero of his youthful novel, *Annette et le criminel,* who himself is derived from a stock type of villain-hero in the novel of terror, with touches of Sir Walter Scott's Cleveland. It would not surprise me if two of Vautrin's most distinguished ancestors were Milton's Satan and Goethe's Mephistopheles; and certainly we see projected in him his creator's suppressed revolt against society. One of Balzac's recent commentators suggests that the origin of most of his characters is conceptual, and goes on to say: "Balzac is an abstract intelligence, inclined rather towards the conception of ideas than the intuition of beings and things."[18] I find myself more in agreement with another critic, who speaks of "the perpetual victory of

18 Ramon Fernandez, *Balzac* (Paris, 1943), p. 37.

his imagination over the abstract."[19] Balzac's characters, however "conceptual" their origin may be, enter as soon as they are born a concrete world in which each achieves a personal and surprising life of its own.

We have seen that all characters are partly defined in relation to social groups, that something of themselves is revealed in their houses, their rooms, in everything that they touch. The clothes they wear or would like to wear cast light upon their personalities: we think of Colonel Chabert in his old frock coat, his "carrick"; we sympathize with the worry of Eugène de Rastignac in his fear of not being suitably dressed to appear before the great ladies of Parisian society, and share at once the dazzlement of Eugènie and the irony of her father before the fashionable appearance of young Charles Grandet. "For in civilized countries," Balzac writes in his *Physiologie de la toilette,* "whoever speaks of *man* speaks of man *fully clothed;* man sprung naked from the hands of nature is, in the existing order of things, unfinished: the tailor is called upon to complete him."[20]

But if his personality is revealed by his houses, his furniture, and his clothes, it is revealed even more by his physical appearance. We need take no more seriously the phrenological or pseudo-biological generalities with which Balzac sometimes weights his portraits than we take his remarks on astrology: it is in spite of, not because of, such references that each character assumes his individual life. We have only to read some phrases from the portraits of three girls—Catherine Tonsard,

[19] Albert Béguin, *Balzac Visionnaire* (Paris, 1946), p. 115.
[20] *Physiologie de la toilette,* XXXIX, 50.

the peasant, Eugénie Grandet, the bourgeoise, and Rosalie de Watteville, the daughter of provincial nobility—to realize the difference in their natures.

Catherine, a tall strong girl, exactly the type that sculptors and painters choose for models of *Liberty,* as they once did for *The Republic,* charmed the youth of the Avonne valley by that same voluminous breast, the muscular legs, the waist at once firm and flexible, the brawny arms, the eye gleaming with a spark of flame, by the proud look, the hair twisted in thick handfuls, the virile brow, the red mouth, the lips drawn back in an almost savage smile, that Eugène Delacroix and David d'Angers have both admirably caught and represented.[21]

Catherine is a simple person: her sensuality, her violence, her independence have all been suggested in this short sketch. Now let us take Eugénie Grandet. The fact that in certain ways she physically resembles Catherine makes the difference all the more striking.

Eugénie had the strong build so often found among children of the *petite bourgeoisie.* Her head was very large; the lines of her forehead, delicate and yet virile, suggested the Jupiter of Phidias; the purity of her life seemed concentrated in the dazzling clearness of her grey eyes. The features of her round face, originally fresh and rosy, had been coarsened by an attack of smallpox mild enough to leave no scars though it had destroyed the bloom of her skin. Her nose was a little too large but it suited the kindly and affectionate expression of her very red mouth.[22]

I have not quoted the whole description, but even

21 *Les Paysans,* XXIII, 204.
22 *Eugénie Grandet,* VIII, 335.

119

these few sentences give us the feeling of Eugénie herself. Eugénie, however, is not so simple a character as Catherine. From this picture of her as a young girl we could not predict the spinsterish woman in her thirties—at once confident and repressed, charitable and shrewd, filled with a sort of impersonal kindness and a secret irony—that she has become by the end of the novel.

Rosalie is as different as possible from both the others:

> At eighteen, Mademoiselle de Watteville was a slight, thin, flat, blond, colorless and utterly insignificant girl. Her pale blue eyes were given a certain interest by the flutter of her long lashes which when she looked down cast a shadow upon her cheeks. A few freckles spotted the whiteness of her forehead, which was rather nicely modeled. Her face was exactly like the faces of Albrecht Dürer's saints and those of the painters before Perugino: the same slender plumpness, the same delicacy saddened by ecstasy, the same stern artlessness.[23]

From this portrait no one would suspect that Rosalie will use the boldest trickery to gratify a stubborn passion for a man whom she has known only by sight. If then in the case of very simple people, like Catherine, the introductory portrait may more or less sum up the personality, in other cases it merely hints at the nature behind it, and sometimes it actually misleads. Always, however, it does at last become part of the character: once we know Rosalie we cannot imagine her with different features. We have learned to interpret them correctly.

[23] *Albert Savarus,* III, 16.

The reader may have noticed that in each of these descriptions Balzac compares his character to some work of art: Catherine suggests an allegorical figure by Delacroix; Eugénie's brow recalls the Phidian Zeus; Rosalie looks like one of Dürer's saints. Balzac often makes such comparisons to give us an over-all physical image, to bring the details together. At times, as in the case of Catherine Tonsard, they add depth and space to the picture: we glimpse her, for a moment, in a red Phrygian cap, at the head of a revolutionary mob. At times their effect depends not only on the *special* resemblance but on the implied *general* difference. When Balzac, to suggest the calm breadth of Eugénie's brow, the massiveness of her head, calls to our minds the statue of Zeus, the image impresses us all the more sharply just because Eugénie in every other way is unlike Zeus. Proust has developed to its utmost the effect of such a comparison in his identification of Odette Swann with a figure by Botticelli.

But we should not gather the impression that Balzac invariably introduces each character by a physical portrait, as if a member of a theatrical cast were stepping upon the scene. He describes his people at the moment when he wants to call our attention to their appearance. Eugénie, for example, is not described until well along in the story, after we already know her and have met most of the other characters; the time Balzac chooses is when, dazzled by the vision of her young cousin from Paris, she looks into the glass and thinks: "I am not beautiful enough for him." Often a person is described on many different occasions to give a sense of his changing: such is the case with Philippe Bridau and Flore

Brazier. But Balzac tells us no more of anyone's appearance than he thinks is necessary for our understanding. If Lucien de Rubempré—with his rather feminine hips, his suggestion of an Indian Bacchus—is pictured at length, the appearance of Eugène de Rastignac, quite as important a character, is given in one short sentence: "Eugène de Rastignac had a southern face, a pale complexion, black hair and blue eyes." All we know of Dinah's appearance is that she is beautiful.

It is true, however, that Balzac's approach to his characters is almost always one that might be described as physical: he begins from the outside, with what is tangible and concrete. If we are shown no precise picture of Dinah or Valérie, as we are of Eugénie and Flore, we none the less can imagine the play of their features, the kind of glances they cast, the movements of their shoulders, the gestures of their hands as they talk. We learn of the characters' ideas or attitudes, sometimes at great length, but as a rule it is only after these have become externalized in the spoken word or in the revealing letters they write to each other. We are told, of course, of Dinah's struggles against provincial pettiness in Sancerre, and then of her passion for Lousteau and the changes it undergoes as she sees him more and more clearly; but such psychological events are not described in a "psychological" manner—by the detailed analysis of what the character is thinking and feeling at this or that special moment. What we are directly told of Dinah's inner struggles is presented swiftly as a narrative summing up of many special moments.

There are of course, as always with Balzac, exceptions: we see Raphaël Valentin at the instant of his vision of the unity of the physical world; we go with Véronique Sauviat on her lonely walk when she becomes aware of the consoling permanence of nature. We are given a touching glimpse of Eugénie Grandet as she notices the sun shining on a patch of the old stone wall of her garden, on the dried grasses, the ferns and bluebells that grow in the crannies; the effect of the light, the faint dry rustle of the leaves become as it were the very expression of her love for Charles, so that after his departure that fragment of wall reminds her of her happiest moments—in something the way that Vinteuil's little phrase recalls to Swann the dawn of his love for Odette.

At times Balzac describes for us experiences that would seem to have nothing to do with the nature of his characters. When Lucien, imprisoned in the Conciergerie, his hopes ruined, is about to kill himself, he has a strange hallucination: through the window of his cell he sees the palace of Louis IX intact before him; it is so real that he wonders how such a marvelous old building can still exist unknown in the heart of Paris. "There were two Luciens, a poet walking through the Middle Ages, beneath the arcades and the turrets of Saint Louis, and a young man preparing for suicide." We might imagine that it is the memory of something Lucien had read in the uncorrupted days of his youth and long ago forgotten, a sense of what he might have been, which now returns to him in this image, apparently quite distinct from himself. There is the burst of ideal music like the finale of Beethoven's *Fifth Sym-*

phony that César Birotteau, the least poetic of men, hears in his moment of triumph after his ball and again just before his death.

Glimpses such as these are exceptions in that they do give the essence of a particular moment; but they are not psychological analyses, like so many of the lucidly probed reveries of Julien Sorel and Fabrice del Dongo. Balzac has rather plunged straight from the surface to below the level of conscious thought and given us, almost lyrically, a moment of direct feeling. Even at such moments the feeling is suggested in physical terms: it is the sunlight that she sees on the patch of wall that becomes a mysterious symbol of Eugénie's happiness; Raphaël's vision of the unity and Véronique's sense of the permanence of nature are inseparable from the actual water and rocks and trees that are before their eyes; Lucien's hallucination comes to him as a visual experience which he mistakes for the image of something really there; César's joy and triumph seem literally, like music, to be ringing in his ears.

6

But in general it is by what they do and, most of all, by what they say, that we come to know Balzac's characters; it is by their mannerisms, their physical ambience, conveyed by a quantity of strokes. "Isn't it alarming," Balzac writes in his *Théorie de la démarche*, "that a keen observer may discover a vice, a remorse, a disease, by watching a man in motion?" As we watch them

124

move and as we listen to them talk, we become penetrated by their essence, and then a miracle occurs:
they are transformed; they assume a special life of
their own. Like some of the great characters of Dickens,
the most extraordinary characters of Balzac—the
"monstres," the "monomanes"—may suggest the
densely black silhouettes of some gigantic puppet show;
but presently we realize that it is only the sharpness
of their outlines that has made them look flat, only the
violence of their movements that has suggested puppets.
They are not unreal but super-real, like figures in a
dream, endowed with a permanence, a continuity that
dreams do not possess. Dickens is apt to plunge us directly into his visionary world: the Wellers, father and
son, and Mr. Pecksniff are their own supernatural
selves from the moment they begin to speak. Balzac's
procedure is somewhat different. He presents his characters at first in the light of day; they solidly establish
themselves as beings of ordinary dimensions, and most
of them, as the story unfolds, try to delude us that they
are still on the same plane as ourselves. But with the
extraordinary cases the transformation sooner or later
becomes clear. Sometimes, as with César Birotteau, it
is a gradual process: it is through a series of desperate
yet trifling actions, of brief dialogues that he assumes
his heroic and fabulous stature. With Lisbeth Fischer,
perhaps we first notice the change in the scene when
Valérie tells her that the young sculptor Wenceslas, her
protégé, her "one lamb out of all the flock," is going
to marry the lovely Hortense; and Lisbeth, unable to
control her trembling, pours out to the startled Valérie
her jealousy, her ferocity, and the pent-up frustration

125

of her whole life. From that moment Lisbeth becomes an avenging fury, all the more frightening because she is able to control outwardly her consuming flame.[24] With Philippe Bridau—the gambler and thief, the ex-officer of Napoleon's army—the change occurs when he reappears, after a term in prison, determined by whatever means to win a fortune. He is no longer just a shoddy ruffian but a kind of infernal genius, endowed with the demonic quality we meet later in the family of the Karamazovs.[25]

This magical intensification or enlargement cannot be illustrated by brief quotations, because it is so much the effect of the whole. Talk, action, the "feel" of the scene, everything penetrates and colors everything else. The ghoulish and gusty Madame Cibot, she too, like Lisbeth and Philippe, possessed by a devil, might be suggested through some of her speeches; but it would require long quotations in the original French, because the marvelous flood of words with which she subdues poor Pons, as he lies helpless and ill, could no more be translated than the conversations of Sairey Gamp.

But it is important to remember that, while becoming in a sense supernatural, Balzac's characters do not lose their naturalness; they rarely sever their contact with ordinary life. As our eyes grow accustomed to their unearthly lighting, we begin to see their roundness, their complexity. Philippe's egotism, for example, is a highly personal mixture of many things: a defense against frustration and disappointment, which is involved not only with his private failure but with the

24 See *La Cousine Bette.*
25 See *La Rabouilleuse.*

126

doom of his hero, Napoleon; a dim feeling that some-
how he must revenge himself against fate; a love of the
sensual life and therefore the need at any cost to place
himself in a position where he can enjoy it; an urge,
which in itself might have been admirable, to make the
most of his talents. We find curious contradictions as
we examine his character: along with his ambition
there is a kind of indifference to what happens to him;
along with his inability to resist grasping at once whatever appeals to him there is the power to plan with cold
deliberation.

Of the dozen or more misers—Grandet, Gobseck, Elie
Magus and the rest—no two are alike; their avarice
is no more a discrete entity than Philippe's egotism.
To take only Grandet as an example: his miserliness
is, of course, partly the thrift of the peasant, an ex-
aggerated desire for security; but it is even more the
lust for power. It is also the product of a kind of ironic
game he likes to play: he is honest, for all his sharpness—that is to say, he keeps within the law—because
if he were not, he would feel that the pleasure would
be gone; it would be like cheating at solitaire. This
miserliness is partly too the eagerness of the collector.
When Eugénie tells him that she has given Charles the
ancient gold coins that Grandet himself had given her
through the years, his shock is of the kind that might
strike a philatelist if his child, in whom he had been
trying to cultivate an interest in stamps, had disposed
of a unique set of postmaster's provisionals. Avarice
comes more and more to dominate him, like the growth
of a chronic disease, but it is always *his own* avarice;
it takes its special color from him, from his peasant

sturdiness, his drily primitive humor, his irony, his pride.

What Balzac gives us by presenting a surface, by showing us each character largely from the outside, is the opposite of a superficial effect. It is the sense of an unfissionable entity endowed with a powerful life of its own, and yet an inseparable and mysterious part of all the life that exists. A surface is never for Balzac merely a surface: it leads indefinitely inward.

On the magic skin that the antique dealer gives to Raphaël there are written some strange signs in an oriental tongue. "Don't you know," asks the old man, "that for the superstitious East the mystical form and the deceptive figures of this emblem represent a fabulous power?" We might say that each of Balzac's characters is, like the emblem inscribed on the piece of skin, to all appearances a tangible and measurable pattern, but a pattern that becomes the symbol of *une puissance fabuleuse*.

7

Balzac's attitude toward his characters might be described as a vast sympathy that neither accuses nor excuses. He has such a grasp of the point of view of each one, of all the attendant, the possibly mitigating circumstances, that, like a wise and disillusioned psychiatrist or priest, he is never shocked. He knows that there is a narrow line between the saint and the sinner, that no one could predict what, under stress of different situations, each might have become. He knows that if pure evil would inevitably be repellent, there is no such thing in life as pure evil—that the evil we meet is often so combined with other elements that the effect may be one of charm and fascination; just as he knows that the most admirable goodness may be combined with other qualities which may repel us or stir us to laughter.

If we sympathize with Abbé Birotteau thrust out of his beloved rooms, we can realize that in spite of his excellent qualities he could be a tactless and irritating person. We disapprove of the heartless behavior of Père Goriot's daughters; but it was their father who originally spoiled them, and we see how, from their point of view, his presence would be often difficult and embarrassing. Abbé Birotteau's stupidity is not a virtue; it is a weakness. So is the blind adoration that Goriot feels for his daughters. When Adeline Hulot offers herself at last to Crevel, to save her family from ruin, Balzac is not describing a pseudo-heroic or saintly action but the aberration of a desperate woman driven through prolonged anxiety to the verge of madness. Adeline Hulot is a good woman, but this action is not a good action: it would be utterly absurd (in a way that Adeline is not) if it did not have the excuse of nervous illness. Any of Balzac's characters, however admirable, may commit weak or foolish actions. Any of them, however weak or base, may surprise us by a show of generosity or courage. Even the contemptible Fraisier, in his ghoulish bargain with Madame la Présidente de Marville, thinks of his friend, the unlucky Dr. Poulain; the ruffian Philippe Bridau keeps to the end the disinterested courage of a soldier. No one, even among the possessed, is cut off from humanity and irrevocably damned.

It is true, however, that Balzac does now and then make moral comments on the actions of his characters. Sometimes he appears to be defending himself against those who accused him of immorality; sometimes he identifies himself, more or less unconsciously, with what he knows to be the popular judgment. But in any case, such comments are by the way; most often they consist of a word, such as "sublime" or "infernal," or a short phrase. The real attitude of a novelist toward his characters is not shown by external comment, for which he may have various reasons, but rather by the whole manner of presentation.

Though Balzac's humor is most often sharpened by irony, few characters are committed to an inevitably ironic treatment. If the inarticulate Monsieur de Bargeton, with his dancer's smile, seems at first merely absurd, no one could be less absurd than he as he challenges to a duel the man who gossiped about his wife. We might assume at first that Dinah de La Baudraye would be regarded with a consistent irony in which her judgment of herself would be slyly contrasted with Balzac's superior judgment. Before long, as we know, she becomes an almost tragic figure whom we look at with no trace of amusement. Our feelings about César Birotteau and many others change in the same way.

Balzac's irony is different from that of Flaubert, whose deliberately detached treatment, in its very insistence upon letting the characters damn themselves out of their own mouths, is actually an interpretation.

Our remarks take on their color, in a sense their meaning, from the general context of the occasion, the mood as felt and created by the participants. But the wonderful Monsieur Homais, as presented and therefore as the reader sees him, is never as he is seen or felt by himself or any of the surrounding characters: it is Flaubert who admirably manipulates him, as he does Jacques Arnoux, so as to reveal in the clearest light how vulgar, how absurd he is. Homais and Arnoux are intensely alive; but they are Flaubert's Homais, Flaubert's Arnoux. If the irony should waver, the character would disappear, because Flaubert cannot imagine his existing under any other light.

Balzac's characters, like his streets and his houses, seem to exist in themselves, independent of the lighting. He may be both amused and touched by Mlle Cormon; he may be both fascinated and appalled by Vautrin; but neither Mlle Cormon nor Vautrin is hampered or limited by any such shifting attitude. It is the people themselves who engross Balzac's attention, and not himself as he watches them. But if he suspends judgment, it is not only because of the warmth of his understanding. It is also because he is aware that no one can penetrate the inmost soul of another, that a character completely defined is not completely living.

One could fancy Balzac, when he created his characters, calling into the dark where his stored experience lay buried, and then tensely waiting, like someone who consults an oracle, for an echo to come back out of the depths. When he caught it at last, he would be surprised by the way the tone of his voice, even the message he had called were transformed, charged with implications, reverberations, whose origin he could not exactly know, whose limits he could not exactly measure. We have the same feeling as we read Dickens or Dostoievski. The unobservable transforming process that takes place within that zone of shadow is what we call the creative imagination.

PART IV

The Telling of the Story

I have undertaken the history of a whole society.
I have often described my plan in this one sentence: "A generation is a drama with four or five
thousand outstanding characters." That drama is
my book.

—*Lettre à Hyppolite Castille*

1

The greatest difference between living people and fictional characters, it would seem to me, is simply that the former exist in real space and time, the latter do not. The task of the novelist, therefore, is to surround his characters with imaginary space and time. Of course the feeling of space may be suggested by the presentation of background—the rooms, the streets, the forests through which the characters move—and by the physical description of the people themselves; but this spatial illusion, in the works of the great novelists, is completed by the ordering of events, by the continual decisions as to what will be revealed, what will be suggested, what will be completely passed over. When critics discuss the pattern in the later novels of Henry James, with its insistence on calculated proportion and the careful adjustment of "the point of view," they sometimes fail to see that it is really a manner of lighting the characters, bathing them in fluid space, as a painter by his arrangement of color and line may steep in air the figures upon his canvas. Henry James does not make use of all of Balzac's means, and those that he chooses he elaborates and refines upon; but no one familiar with both Henry James and Balzac can be surprised by the younger novelist's tribute to his master: "I speak of him," James writes in *The Lesson of Balzac,* "and can only speak, as a man of his own craft, an emulous fellow worker, who has learned from him

135

more of the lessons of the engaging mystery of fiction than from any one else."

If the sense of space is created by the interplay of various means, the sense of time depends almost entirely upon proportion and arrangement. It is as if events were uprooted from the medium in which they always exist, like fronds of seaweed torn from the water that supports them so that they lie in a flat tangle upon the sand, and then as if the novelist had to rearrange them so that they might give us the illusion of still swaying with the drift of the tide—still each one naturally expanded in the living submarine forest or garden. One of the novelist's hardest tasks is this rearrangement, this attempt to catch time between the covers of a book. It is the sense of time and space—together with the drama or plot, which can only develop in terms of time and space—that is created by the telling of the story.

That is why I consider the story of immense importance and cannot follow those austere critics who dismiss it as a regrettable necessity. The narration of a series of happenings, no matter how simple, no matter how tenuous the causal relationship between them (and succession most often implies causality which, if not stressed, may become only the more exciting), has always charmed the mind of man if it has been presented with the art to arouse curiosity and suspend disbelief. I am sure it always will. Plot and pattern, the highest sophistications of form in the novel, are developments of the way a story is told; character and event were originally and remain ultimately inseparable. The prince and the princess in a fairy tale are simple crea-

136

tions; but the child who listens to the tale must believe in their existence, just as he must believe in Red Riding Hood and the wolf. So, conversely, in even the most serious novel the characters are in a measure what they do. Nor do I see how we can draw a line between what they *do* and what they think or feel: for events are not merely external happenings. A shock of joy or grief is an event just as much as a birth or a death. The excitement of Little Red Riding Hood comes not only from her finding the wolf in her grandmother's bed but from her fear as she realizes that it *is* the wolf and not her grandmother.

Part of the picture of the charming and touching Milly Theale in *The Wings of the Dove* is her visit to the great doctor, Sir Luke Strett, her falling in love with Merton Densher, her "turning her face to the wall" when she is told by Lord Mark of the plot that has been woven about her, and the fact that, in spite of her knowledge, she none the less bequeaths Densher her fortune. We cannot separate our idea of Anna Karenina from her flight with Vronsky and her flinging herself under the train. *Ulysses* and *A la Recherche du temps perdu* have been held up as examples of novels from which the story element has been almost completely banished. Yet, as we know, *Ulysses* is a transposition into modern dress of one of the most delightful stories ever told: its interest depends just as much on Bloom's and Stephen's meeting, on the final homecoming to Marion Bloom, as the Odyssey depends on the meeting of Telemachus and Odysseus and the return to Penelope. *A la Recherche du temps perdu* is a whole network of stories, a modern *Arabian*

137

Nights; though, unlike the *Arabian Nights,* the stories are all subordinated to one dominating pattern. We want to find out what happens, and little by little we see what happens to Marcel and Gilberte and Albertine, to Monsieur de Charlus and Morel, to Madame Verdurin and the Duchesse de Guermantes.

Of course in these novels there is a marked shift in the proportion of outer and inner events, although the difference between them and, let us say, *Tom Jones* is not perhaps so much in the number of outer events as in the manner in which they are told us. The long section of *Du Côté de chez Swann,* for example, that describes Marcel's life as a boy in Combray and that might be considered uneventful, contains many such events—the meetings with Bloch and Legrandin and Gilberte, Marcel's call upon his uncle where he sees the lady in pink (whose real identity, as in a mystery story, is not revealed until later), his peering through the window at Mlle Vinteuil and her friend; but these events are not related in chronological order. They are told long after they have occurred, as we see them reflected in his memory. The device, by the way, of wrapping events in a mysterious and special reality by speaking of them as if they had happened long ago is something we find in the most naive tales, with their opening formula of "once upon a time." One might even think of Proust's long novel as an infinitely complex and subtle elaboration of that formula.

To speak of the absence of "story," then, in even the most sophisticated or psychological novel seems to me like speaking of the lack of melody in a Bach fugue. If we cannot hum a fugue as we can a pure song, it is

138

because there are a number of voices set one against the other, because their interweaving is so complex, because we cannot separate the melodic from the harmonic structure any more than we can separate, in a great novel, story and characterization. If sometimes our memory of the character is sharper than our memory of what happened to him, that does not alter the fact that our knowledge of him in the first place was often gathered from what happened to him: the particular events have faded, like skillfully presented parts, into our impression of the whole which could not exist without them.

Balzac was not only concerned with his characters as things in themselves: he was equally concerned with making them move, as all life must, through space and time. He was fascinated by the telling of the story. Even a glance at his revisions, his amplifications and abridgements, his shifts in the order of parts, and finally the means he used to combine his separate novels into one all-enveloping story would make this clear. The actual beginning of *Le Curé de Tours,* for example, was only arrived at after sixteen rejected tries.[1]

Although the novel is the least conventionalized of genres, we find that even among novelists there are those who, for their own purposes, have arrived at certain forms as desirable and have allowed this preconception to determine the shape or the texture of the book. Flaubert, of course, had fixed theories about style, so that—whether he was writing of modern Paris or ancient Carthage—whatever he wrote was the ex-

---

[1] See *The Evolution of Balzac's Comédie humaine* (ed. Dargan and Weinberg; Chicago, 1941), which contains, among other revealing studies, "Variations in *Le Curé de Tours,*" by Rachel Wilson.

pression of the same stylistic ideal. We can no more conceive of Henry James's putting a paragraph from the point of view of Madame de Vionnet or Chad Newsome into the text of *The Ambassadors* (consecrated to presenting, at least directly, only what Strether can perceive) than we can think of Flaubert's leaving an assonance or the repetition of a word that called attention to itself.

Balzac, like Tolstoi or Dostoievski, would not belong to this group. If he paid the greatest attention to the shape he gave to each of his stories, it was a shape that grew out of the nature of the story itself. The constant remodelings, the continuous revisions from the proofs suggest not only that he was eager to find the most suitable form but also that his idea of what the form should be was sometimes arrived at gradually and gropingly. There is no single technical principle beneath the shaping of his stories that would correspond to the general manner in which he approaches his characters, although, of course, that very approach to character affects the shape of the stories and is (as indeed everything is) a part of the manner of their telling.

2

For a long time one of the stock remarks to make about Balzac was that he wrote badly; one still hears it, though not so often. Even from the first there were those who, refusing to judge his style by the standard of classical French prose, realized the force, the variety, and above all the vitality of his writing. Taine and Gautier, neither of whom can be said to have had no feeling for language, were among that number. Like everything having to do with form, style for Balzac was a means to an end. Flaubert insisted that his own style, whatever it might express, should have in itself a quality which he thought of as "beauty." For him this meant a carefully arranged cadence, a certain deliberate music whereby the sound of the word or phrase should reinforce the sense. When sound and sense merge, they produce an effect at once firm and brilliant shot through with a kind of lyrical suggestiveness that is yet presented in strictly prose terms, an effect that no other novelist quite achieves. But at times, especially in *Madame Bovary,* the deliberateness of the effort may give us a queer feeling that we are watching a masquerade.[2]

Neither Balzac nor Stendhal had any idea of creating a kind of abstract beauty by his manner of writing. If we are looking for harmony, evenness, or purity of style, we should not turn to *La Comédie humaine.* One cannot give an adequate idea of a style without citing instances, and these, naturally, lose their point if translated; so I shall not attempt a stylistic analysis of Balzac. There is perhaps no great writer from whose works it is easier to pick out unfortunate phrases. In *Une Double Famille,* for example, Caroline's little girl wakes up in the night "demandant sa limpide nourriture." But it is when Balzac begins lecturing us that his writing is most apt to become stilted or turgid. On

---

[2] For a neat illustration of differences between Balzac's and Flaubert's styles, see B. F. Bart, "Balzac and Flaubert, Energy versus Art," *Romanic Review,* XLII (October, 1951), 198-204.

the other hand, he is at his best when he is speaking through someone else: Madame Cibot or Madame Vauquer, Père Grandet or Père Goriot. Then, of course, the style is no longer his; it is the living speech of a hundred different characters; and if he can find for them all a wonderful spate of words, he can also charge with horror, humor, or pathos the shortest and simplest phrase. We may take as an example César Birotteau's, "Je ne suis pas bien," when with the ideal music—the faraway memory of his one triumphant evening—still ringing in his ears, he is too near death to realize that he is dying. Often there is not the definite boundary line one would expect between Balzac's own style and that of his characters. As Bardèche points out, "Balzac listens to his characters with such insistence that he loses his neutrality as a narrator and his style, the better to describe them, reflects their speech."[3] We might on occasions compare his banality or flatness of phrase, his awkwardness or pompousness, with Joyce's use of the sentimental cliché and of the heavy "tired" style in the chapters of *Ulysses* where Bloom on the twilit beach notices Gerty Macdowell or looks in, late at night, at the cabman's shelter. With Joyce, however, the device is sustained and deliberate; with Balzac it is incidental and most often, no doubt, unconscious.

As Gautier realized, Balzac does not hesitate to pick his vocabulary or his metaphors from any source; he makes use of "every kind of technical term, every kind of slang, scientific, artistic, theatrical." If most often, except when his characters speak, the expression does not strike us as "inevitable," it may suggest to us some-

[3] Maurice Bardèche, *Balzac, Romancier* (Paris, 1940), p. 557.

thing of the indeterminacy of life itself. Everything might have happened just a little differently from the way it did happen; how can we be sure that what seems to happen in a certain way did, in fact, happen in precisely that way? Too tight and deliberate a style may seem to constrict movement: either it happened in exactly the manner I describe it, the writer seems to assert, or it did not happen at all. Sometimes we may take his word for it, and our vision coincides with his. Sometimes, however, we may simply not believe him, and reply with a certain defiance: "Very well, then: for us it did not happen, at least not in itself. It was you who contrived it."

There is in Balzac's writing a tremendous freedom and sweep, a constant element of surprise. We know from his correspondence that he often felt baffled in his struggle to find words. We can see from a glance into any of his novels that he was sometimes defeated, though we can also see, from passages of clear, sharp, and eloquent writing, that he was often triumphant. But even such passages lose in being quoted: no more than the awkward or tasteless passages can they be considered separately. They exist as their real selves only in relation to the entire context.

3

Baudelaire speaks of Balzac's "prodigious taste for detail," and we cannot read one of his novels or stories without noticing it for ourselves. "People who insist upon immediate interest," he remarks in *Les Paysans,* "will say my explanations are too long." In the Preface to the first edition of the *Scènes de la Vie privée,* he writes: "The author firmly believes that details alone will henceforth determine the merit of works improperly called novels"—improperly so called because the term *roman* might suggest something frivolous. What Balzac wants to do is to show us the very process of human activity. At any cost he must convince us. After the long explanation of Rabourdin's plan to simplify the bureaucratic system of the government, he comments: "You would not take the narrator at his word, if he merely affirmed the talent and the initiative of a *chef de bureau.*"[4]

Such passages inform us not only that he was quite aware of what he was doing, but also that he realized its dangers. When he wanted to tell an anecdote for its own sake, he could be as bare and swift as Mérimée; I think especially of the remarkable group of very short stories in *Conversation entre onze heures et minuit.*[5] But as a rule the effect he is seeking depends on elaboration. What saves *La Messe de l'athée,* for example, from being merely a pleasant, rather sentimental anecdote is the leisurely and spacious way in which it is told. Superficially, it is a kind of mystery story constructed like one of the adventures of Sherlock Holmes: we are presented with a surprising fact and finally the

[4] *Les Employés,* XIX, 22.

[5] These stories appeared in 1832 as Balzac's contribution to *Contes bruns,* a collection which also contained stories by two of his friends. Some parts of the *Conversation* Balzac used later in *La Comédie humaine;* what he did not use he renamed *Echantillon de causerie française,* published in 1844. He had planned to include this in a future edition of *La Comédie humaine,* but did not live to do so. The main character in one of the stories, a ruffianly lieutenant colonel who had served under Napoleon, might be the first sketch of Philippe Bridau.

explanation, which we could not have guessed, is revealed. But with Balzac what is important is not the surprise ending; it is rather the necessity of convincing us that a person may perform an action quite inconsistent with his beliefs. *Madame Firmiani* and *L'Interdiction* have the same mystery element: in each case strange and possibly immoral behavior proves to be admirable and understandable. In both these tales, also, character and story are one.

But it is in the novels that the use of detail is most striking. It is the living density of their texture that makes us believe in the real existence of the streets and houses, of the fields and towns, of the society from which the characters emerge, and of those characters themselves. We know the Maison Vauquer as well as any of the boarders could know it; we know the general "tone" of the boarders as a group because we have been shown each one so carefully; and knowing this we can get the full effect of Père Goriot's social decadence and can sympathize with Eugène's efforts to break away. We know equally well Dinah's surroundings in Sancerre; we see just how they have helped mold her character and how, like Eugène, she is driven to escape from them. By the time Philippe Bridau arrives in Issoudun to begin his murderous campaign, we have completely the feeling of the town, of the cliques that inhabit it, with their feuds, their interests, and their prejudices; and so we are able to appraise the skill with which Philippe takes advantage of all such things.

Sometimes the detail is used to emphasize the central theme of the story. In reading *La Recherche de l'absolu* for the first time, we may wonder why the house should be so minutely described. It is only after finishing the book that we see how the densely crowded picture of that house, with so much that has come down from the past, sharpens the contrast with the mad dispersal of what had taken so long to accumulate. *Les Paysans* begins with a detailed description of the château of Aigues, its gardens and its vast park. As we first read it, we cannot be aware of how that picture sets off the misery of the surrounding peasants, how the lovely dreamlike place will soon become a fortress withstanding the most ominous and persistent siege. The structure of the book demands that as we read about the peasants we keep a positive sense of the château: it is like a prolonged organ point without which the whole superstructure of thematic material would lose much of its meaning.

Balzac has then a genius for imagining detail and the art of making it coalesce into the massive blocks out of which his novels are built; but he does not always succeed in avoiding the danger of which he was himself aware. The reader must force his way at times through cluttered and obscure trails.

Most often this is the result of Balzac's entire belief in the reality of his own characters. Massimilla Doni becomes so fascinated, and Balzac with her, in analyzing Rossini's *Moses* for a visiting Frenchman that she continues, with few breaks, for some twenty pages; Gambara lovingly describes his own opera act by act; we are forced to read Lucien's complete review of the play in which Florine and Coralie appear. We should be glad to take Balzac's word for most of this. In fact

146

we should much prefer to have merely a sample of *Moses;* the first act, let us say, of Gambara's opera; and a paragraph or so from Lucien's article. But for Balzac as he writes, Gambara's opera and Lucien's article become as important and exciting as they are to Gambara or Lucien (because for the moment he *is* Gambara or Lucien) and he cannot resist the temptation to go on and on, just as the characters themselves would do if they could buttonhole a listener. Meanwhile our attention wanders and we feel in something the position of the wedding guest waylaid by the Ancient Mariner. I am afraid that few but the confirmed Balzaciens will reach the end of *Les Employés,* in spite of its brilliant picture of bureaucratic life, and many must have denied themselves the great experience of reading *Illusions perdues* because they were discouraged by the minute historical description of the printing business in the first part.

Sometimes even when there is a definitely structural purpose for the piling on of detail, it defeats itself by its very exuberance. In *Le Cabinet des antiques,* just before the climax (a trial in which the son of the oldest family in a provincial town is acquitted although guilty of forgery), Balzac pauses to give an account of the different lawyers involved, their relationships, and even their houses, which covers more than twenty pages. Balzac makes us see, by explaining the political setup of the town, just how and why the young man is acquitted; but if we are not very patient, we may have left the courtroom without waiting for the verdict.

Le Curé de village has been condemned by some critics as being formless. Actually, as others have realized, it is one of Balzac's greatest novels, not only for what it contains but for the originality of the construction. There are, however, two passages which no doubt help explain the failure to grasp its true form. The heroine, Véronique Sauviat, eager to reclaim the wilderness of her huge estate as an act of atonement for a criminal passion, is trying to find an agricultural engineer who can do the job. An old friend writes her a letter of three pages enclosing another letter written by a young engineer, Gérard, whom he recommends. After we have read the first two or three pages of this enclosure, we may glance ahead to see how many more there are; and when we discover that there are still a dozen before us, we cannot help wishing that the young man were not so articulate. But this is not all. We have hardly recovered from the effect of the letter, when Gérard becomes involved with a group of village notables in a discussion of the recent July Revolution for fifteen pages more. Gérard's letter convinces us that he is capable of carrying through the task he is about to undertake; his conversation with the doctor and mayor sets Véronique's private tragedy in historical perspective. But we lose sight of Véronique herself for so long that it is only the extraordinary drive of the central theme that holds the novel together.

There is still another kind of obstruction the reader sometimes encounters: I mean Balzac's habit of commenting upon the situation he has imagined. In the midst of Lucien de Rubempré's strange vision, just before his suicide, Balzac remarks: "Today medicine is so willing to admit the phenomena of hallucinations that this mirage of our senses, this strange faculty of our minds, can no longer be questioned." Then he dis-

148

cusses its possible causes in a dozen more lines. The reader completely believes in the hallucination. Balzac does not drag it in as the result of any theory; it must have come to him intuitively as he identified himself in those moments with the defeated and crushed young man. But after he has created it, he looks at it in surprise, wonders how he thought of it and how it may be explained. Balzac's supplementary explanations, even when not in themselves ponderous, rarely add to our belief in the reality of what he is explaining. They are more apt to make us impatient and thereby diminish or destroy that belief.

4

Perhaps even more disturbing to some readers than the thickets of detail is the kind of sensationalism that we call melodrama. Any objection to the sensational in itself (except a personal preference: "I don't like that kind of subject") is no more valid in the case of Balzac than in the case of Dostoievski. Both novelists realized that our ideas of probability are often the result of the narrow range of our experience, the habit of assuming that the routine lives we live most of the time are a general pattern of what all life must normally be. But detectives or criminals do put on disguises; murder and blackmail are violent activities; the most degraded characters do occasionally act upon impulses for good with an effect as startling as the sudden disclosure of evil.

It is still more unreasonable to object to the extraordinary "story interest" that fascinates the reader once he has entered into so many of Balzac's novels. We follow the schemes of Madame Cibot or Cousine Bette or Philippe Bridau with such excitement because we are convinced of the reality of the schemers, just as we are convinced of the reality of Cousin Pons, the Hulot family, of Flore and Max, the people against whom they are plotting. "How many of Balzac's novels are the story of a conspiracy!" Le Breton exclaims; and he deplores the fact. Yet it seems to me that the tracking down of someone, the closing of a net around him, is a matter of legitimate and serious interest, if we know the hunter and the hunted. It is true that, as we read on in *La Rabouilleuse,* Philippe's evil power looms larger and larger until he becomes a figure in a nightmare. We may have the same feeling about Madame Cibot as she waits, like one of Goya's fat old witches, for the death of poor Pons, or even about Mlle Gamard as she plans to oust the Abbé Birotteau from his beloved rooms and rob him of his furniture. But in each of these cases Balzac is giving us the sense of ominous and indefinite evil that any one of us may feel when, in however prosaic and limited way, he is attacked. We are involved, for example, in a minor traffic accident. Presently we receive a threatening notice from the lawyer of the other party. If we think that we are innocent victims of an ambulance chaser, the fear of huge damages, the mere sense of being unfairly harassed may make that other driver and his lawyer—unscrupulous, no doubt, but surely not diabolic—haunt our days and nights as the incarnation of all the evil and all the danger in the universe.

150

Balzac most nearly approaches true melodrama when he turns to writing a thriller, as he does in *L'Histoire des Treize,* with its framework of the mysterious Thirteen, "fraternally bound together and yet strangers before the eyes of the world; who would meet each other like conspirators, at night, sharing their most secret thoughts as they shared a fortune as huge as the Old Man of the Mountain's; their feet in every drawing room, their hands in every safe, their elbows in the streets, their heads on every pillow."[6] As the allusion to the Old Man of the Mountain might suggest, Balzac starts off quite irresponsibly telling a story for its own sake; and we could imagine his placing these tales, along with several others, in a group by themselves and labeling them (as Graham Greene modestly labels some of his splendid yarns) "entertainments." But Balzac cannot make any such sharp division. De Marsay, for example, a recurrent figure in the *Comédie,* is the hero of *La Fille aux yeux d'or.* The Duchesse de Langeais is a friend of Madame de Beauséant's. The Duchesse becomes such a real figure of a coquette, the mysterious affair between de Marsay, Paquita, and the Marquise de San-Réal becomes such a grim evocation of perverse sensuality, that we cannot help taking them seriously; and so, believing in the Duchesse and in Paquita, we may be jarred by the exuberant fictional device of the Thirteen: what we feel is a mixture of genres. That Balzac, however, is aware of what he is doing is suggested by a note at the end of the Béchet edition. After Paquita has been stabbed to death, he writes: "If anybody is interested in *La Fille aux yeux*

[6] *L'Histoire des Treize,* XIII, 8.

d'or, he can see her after the curtain has fallen on the play, like one of those actresses who, to accept their transitory wreaths, get up from the floor in perfect health after being publicly stabbed. Today the girl with the golden eyes is thirty years old and rather faded."[7] Not to admit, however, that such works are inferior would be unfair to Balzac, who depended on no such obvious strangeness to suggest the essential mystery of our lives.

We find also at times, in works that have none of the fantastic nature of *Les Treize,* a sudden piling up of coincidence that annoys us because it is gratuitous. At the end of *La Vendetta,* at the very instant when the old Corsican Barthomeo di Piombo has decided to forgive his daughter for marrying a family enemy, her husband arrives with a lock of her hair, to tell him that she has died of hunger, and an instant later drops dead himself. Such a clumsy "curtain" tends to destroy the credibility and interest of all that has gone before. Even more distressing is the confused series of events at the end of the second part of *Splendeurs et misères des courtisanes.* The lawyer Derville finds out by chance that the famous courtesan La Torpille, mistress of Lucien de Rubempré, is none other than Esther Gobseck for whom he has been searching as the heiress of seven million francs, and the discovery is made just *not* in the nick of time to save both Esther and Lucien from suicide. The novel is full of such brilliant passages that Balzac's sacrifice of plausibility, his straining for the most obvious effects, seems deliberately perverse.

[7] *Etudes de moeurs* in *Scènes de la Vie parisienne* (Paris, 1835), IV, 108.

Perhaps it was when driven by his work and yet unable to stop because of his obligations that, in moments of exhaustion, he fell back on this or that trick he had learned in his youth. The surprising thing is not that such lapses occur but that they do not occur more often.

And yet, with Balzac, the moment one has damned a passage one thinks of extenuations, justifications. In *Splendeurs et misères,* for example, which Balzac refers to in his letters as "comique," he might be suggesting with macabre irony the almost farcical piling up of ill luck upon poor Lucien, once the tide of his fortune has turned. What really has brought about his ruin is not a series of chance events but the mixture of superficiality, vanity, and selfishness in his character. We might defend the intruding bits in *Le Curé de village* by noting a certain parallelism between Gérard's position, as he outlines it in his long letter, and Véronique's, and by saying that the very fact of our losing sight of her for so long increases the effect of the last pages where she is revealed with a sharper clarity than ever before. The more we study the works of the truly great, the more we realize how hard it is to separate strength from weakness. We begin to see that a minutely analytic approach to the mystery of great art, if it may help us to understand it in terms of this or that aspect, must always be tentative and, if it is not aware of its limitations, may well be presumptuous; that what in a lesser man would be a weakness, what in a great man, looked at *in itself,* might appear a weakness, may when viewed in relation to the whole become a source of strength. If Balzac's creative identification with his characters had not led him at times to overtreatment, if his sense of the mystery that is beneath the most expected behavior had not tempted him to play with the violence of the unexpected, his greatest work might not possess its hallucinatory power. One would hesitate, even if it were possible, to tamper with the faults of genius. It would be like destroying the ecological balance of some teeming and fertile land.

5

When we consider the structure of Balzac's novels, there are such a number of different effects, each one obtained by appropriate means, that it is impossible in a few pages to give more than a general idea of the way he subordinates his swarming detail to the overall shape of the story. "However numerous the accessories and the characters may be," he writes in his *Lettres sur la Littérature,* "a novelist should group them according to their importance, subordinate them to the sun of his system, whether it be an interest or a hero, and lead them like a brilliant constellation in a certain order."[8] And again: "I love simple subjects; they show great vigor of conception and are always rich in possibilities." In spite of the number of accessories and characters, Balzac's subjects are most often basically simple; order and unity are achieved, even though the struggle to reach them may have left its trace. I shall discuss first Balzac's pattern of revelation and concealment, what might be called his suggestion of space, and

[8] *Lettres sur la Littérature,* XL, 277.

then some of the ways he deals with the passing of time.

The structure of a Balzac novel is an arrangement of lighted surfaces minutely rendered and pits of suggestive shadow. At first glance, noticing the detailed treatment of the objects in full light, we may think: here is a solid realist; he leaves nothing to the imagination. But presently, as our eye is attracted to the shadows, we realize that it is largely they that give meaning to the picture, that the lighted planes are often used as screens to suggest what may be existing in the spaces they conceal. Just as the climax of a piece of music, the very heart of the meaning, may be expressed by a pause, a silence, so the inmost center of a story may not be put into words. To illustrate Balzac's manner of lighting, I have chosen *Le Colonel Chabert,* a tale simple in structure and not too long, so that we may be able to look at it rather carefully.

The first scene shows us the office of Maître Derville, the lawyer, with its group of lively young clerks. A dilapidated old man appears who will tell his business to none but Derville himself, and Derville is not there. He gives his name as Chabert; and when one of the clerks facetiously asks him if he is the famous Colonel Chabert who was killed at the battle of Eylau, he replies simply, "I am, monsieur." In recalling the episode, we should be apt to think that Chabert was presented as the clerks see him, but actually Balzac does not take us into their minds any more than he does into Chabert's. The scene is wholly dramatic. Chabert's contrast with the mischievous young men gives us a sense of his strangeness, his loneliness, his decadence.

The next scene takes place that evening when Cha-

155

bert calls on Derville. It is now that we learn, through conversation, that the Colonel, officially reported dead, received a head wound resulting in amnesia. When his memory returned, no one would believe his story, and for years he was shut up in an asylum in Germany. His wife married again; she is now the fashionable Comtesse Ferraud; she will neither see him nor answer his letters. Chabert explains that he is living in the hope of vengeance and asks help in establishing his rights. Though the effect of the dialogue is to present Chabert as Derville sees him, the only direct glimpses into Derville's mind are the bare statements that Derville "forgot his client's painful situation as he heard the tale of his past misfortunes," and that Chabert's story "finally convinced Derville and touched him deeply." As for Chabert himself, when Derville accepts his story, Balzac says: "The young lawyer's words were like a miracle to this man rejected for the last ten years by his wife, by justice, by the whole world of society." When he leaves Derville's rooms, with some money Derville loaned him, " 'I can now smoke cigars,' he said to himself." Except for these meager comments this episode is also entirely scenic.

There is now a break of three months. The next scene starts when Chabert's papers arrive bearing out his story. Derville discovers him living in a wretched shack in the suburbs of Paris with an old fellow-soldier. " 'Here's where the man who turned the tide of the battle of Eylau is living!' Derville said to himself, taking in at a glance the whole sordid spectacle." In the course of the scene there are only one or two other short glimpses of Derville's consciousness; there are half a dozen lines that takes us into Chabert's: "When he realized the labyrinth of difficulties in which he would be involved and how much money it would take to struggle through them, the poor soldier received a deadly blow in that power peculiar to mankind that we call the *Will*. He could not bear the thought of going to law; it seemed a thousand times simpler to remain a poor man, a beggar."[9] Derville tries to hearten him, and leaves him to call on the Comtesse. We too leave Chabert and go with Derville.

Balzac tells us then in several pages about the situation of the Comtesse and her present husband, and why she might have reason to fear Chabert's claims. This is in general what Derville is thinking about, as he rides along in the cab, but Balzac does not show us the ordering of his thoughts: he merely tells us the facts we should know and thus takes us for the first time into the enemy's camp. The scene between Derville and the Comtesse is short and pointed; Derville arranges for her to meet her husband in his office a week from that time.

The account of that meeting is the crucial scene of the story: the antagonists, Chabert and his wife, are now face to face, and from this point until the climax the narrative is continuous—that is to say, no longer broken up into separate scenes by intervening gaps of time; we never lose sight of Chabert. Derville tells him that the Comtesse has recognized him although she has denied it. As Chabert leaves the office, the Comtesse waylays him, asks him to ride home with her, uses all her art to arouse his generosity, and after three days,

[9] *Le Colonel Chabert*, VII, 43.

whose passing is told in a few lines, she induces him to offer to disappear. When she shows her hand for an instant, we are given Chabert's reaction in a probing phrase: "He cast on his wife a look that made her blush; she lowered her eyes, and he was afraid he would be forced to despise her." The climax is reached when Chabert, unwilling to sign a preposterous paper presented to him by his wife's lawyer, overhears them plotting to have him committed as insane. Then in a dozen lines Balzac shows us his discouragement, his disgust, his momentary uncertainty; but it is only in his speech to her that we see how the very force of his contempt, his total disillusion have given him his moment of triumph. "Live in peace on the strength of my word," he tells her; "it is better than the scribblings of all the lawyers in Paris. I'll never again claim the name that perhaps I have honored. I'm just a poor devil called Hyacinth who only asks for his place in the sun."[10] He leaves her then; and Balzac says: "Chabert in fact disappeared."

But this is not the end. Derville runs across him months later in the Palais de Justice where Chabert is being given a prison sentence for vagrancy and once more, this time after some years, when he finds him by chance in the public poorhouse. Derville is with Godeschal, one of his former clerks, who had been in his office when Chabert first called. Then, Balzac says, "Derville told him the story you have just heard." "What a fate!" Derville exclaims at the end. "Starting life in an institution for foundlings, he comes back to die in the Home for the Aged, having in the mean-

[10] *Ibid.*, p. 72.

158

while helped Napoleon conquer Egypt and Europe."
In the short account of these last meetings there is not
even a phrase that takes us into Derville's mind.

I have gone through this story at such length to
show in detail Balzac's method. There is first a group
of short scenes with gaps between them—we could
think of them as the tops of submarine hills appearing like scattered islands above the surface of the un-
revealed; then when Chabert and his wife confront each
other, there is, as it were, in the center of this island
chain an unbroken plateau—the swift acting out of the
drama—and again the blank spaces of the ocean, with
the two last islands hardly more than small bare rocks
on the edge of the horizon.

In a way *Le Colonel Chabert* is a psychological story,
for its center is what goes on in Chabert's mind; and
part of its power comes from the skill with which Balzac makes us realize this, in spite of the dramatic quality
of the incidents. Three times Chabert is willing to re-
nounce his identity, and each time the motive of his
renunciation marks a stage in his development: first it
is through weakness and fatigue; next for the sake of
his former love; and last through moral contempt and
a bitter exaltation. Yet the manner of telling is not psychological. Of the seventy-odd pages, all the sentences
that "go behind," as Henry James would say, would
not take up much more than a single page. It is as if
Balzac cast a needle of light across Chabert's consciousness, like the beam of a lighthouse that picks out wave
or cliff from the surrounding blackness, and then left
the reader free to create most of what is there from his
own imagination. Colonel Chabert springs to life from

159

the printed page, he moves, he casts a shadow, precisely because he is not caught in print but suggested between the lines. This effect of moving through space is intensified by what might be called a double manner of presentation. There are several crucial scenes in which Derville does not take part; and yet when we finish the story we have the feeling that we have seen not only our own Chabert but Derville's. The reason no doubt is that Balzac makes us see Derville himself so clearly, that as Chabert sinks into the darkness of his decline we are shown him only on the occasions when Derville meets him, that Balzac mentions at the end that Derville has told his story to the clerk Godeschal. It is as if we were looking through a stereopticon, where two pictures taken from slightly different angles fuse into one to produce an effect of three dimensions. Colonel Chabert, as we recall him, marches to his doom surrounded by the fluid air of history.

I am not suggesting that all of Balzac's stories or novels follow this pattern. What strikes us most about their form, I might repeat, is its variety, its adaptability to the nature of the subject. But in nearly all, depth is achieved by presenting characters at once directly and obliquely. The structure of *Le Curé de village* gives us the effect of the simultaneous existence of two stories—one fully lighted, one that never emerges from the shadow. When we have finished the book we realize that this second one is the *real* story: it exists for us, just because it has not been told, with an unlimited power of suggestion, an unmarred intensity.

6

Le Colonel Chabert and *Le Curé de village* are, like most of Balzac's stories, told in the third person. Sometimes, however, he interposes a narrator between the story and the reader. In the Preface to the first edition of *Le Lys dans la vallée,* the longest work written in this manner, he says:

In several fragments of his work the author has created a character who tells the story in his own name. To arrive at the truth, writers use whatever literary device seems capable of giving the greatest intensity of life to their characters. It was this wish to make their works seem lifelike that caused the greatest men of the last century to choose the prolixity of the novel in letters. First person narration probes the human heart as deeply and yet is more concise. To each work its own form.[11]

Balzac, with his eagerness to try all possible means, has written one long novel, *Mémoires de deux jeunes mariées,* entirely in the form of letters. When he introduces a narrator, it is most often to put a veil between the reader and the story and so, particularly if it deals with strangeness or violence, to prevent its atmosphere from escaping into the humdrum air that we breathe most of the time. *La Grande Bretèche* is a fine example of this. Horace Bianchon tells the story to a group gathered late at night in the *salon* of Mlle des Touches; but he tells it in fragments, as he has pieced

[11] *Oeuvres complètes de Balzac* (Paris: Michel Lévy, 1872), XXII, 428.

it together from his talks with three different people, each one closer to the shocking event which is at last revealed. The event itself we see only indirectly, from far away. If it seems incredible, that may be because one of the intervening narrators has overlooked or distorted something in the telling. But we must be content with our one disturbing glimpse.

I might mention also *Honorine,* longer, more complex, and far more profound. It is an extraordinary probing of the cruelty of a sexual obsession told years afterwards by a narrator who, though deeply involved in the drama, never clearly understands it and who includes in his own account the narrative of another man even more deeply affected than he. The center of the story is the mind of Honorine, the heroine and victim; but our nearest approach to a direct glimpse of that is two of her letters which the narrator reads to his audience. We have an impression of depth below depth of shadow.[12]

Of various other possible examples I shall discuss only one: the full-length novel, *Le Lys dans la vallée.* It begins with a letter from Félix de Vandenesse to his mistress, Natalie de Manerville, in which he tells her that he is going to give her an account of the one great love of his youth, his passion for Madame de Mortsauf who is now dead. Nearly all the rest of the novel is his story as he writes it for Natalie. It is obvious that Félix is one of the characters who share many of Balzac's feelings, that even some of the details of his childhood

---

[12] William Faulkner, who like several other novelists of strikingly original genius would appear to have enriched his art through his creative understanding of Balzac, has made fine use of this kind of indirect presentation—in *Absalom, Absalom,* for example.

reflect Balzac's own; but it is also clear that Félix is not Balzac and that he is writing under great emotional stress. It has been said that Balzac took special pains with the style of this book, not always with fortunate results, that he wanted it to be a kind of diploma piece. I do not deny this, but it seems to me only to support my contention. If Balzac did wish to give an example of how sensitive or "delicate" he could be, what would be more natural than that he should choose a narrator to whom such a manner, at once more "elegant" and more flushed than Balzac's usual manner, would be appropriate?

Balzac obviously sympathizes with Félix and his love for Madame de Mortsauf (which reflects no doubt his own feeling for Madame de Berny), but he also regards him with a certain irony. That Félix's writing Natalie about his love is not a merely formal device is proved, I think, by the constant references to Natalie ("Here, Natalie"; "Shall I confess to you, Natalie?" and many others) so that the reader can never forget that this is Félix's narrative written for a special person, by Madame de Mortsauf's letter which shows him after her death that he had not fully understood her temperament, and by Natalie's final comment on his manuscript, which tells him very pointedly that he has never understood his own. "Poor woman," she writes of Madame de Mortsauf, "she certainly suffered, and now that you have concocted a few sentimental phrases, you think you have cleared all accounts with her tomb." Félix's story, in other words, is not the whole story. It reveals to us much of what happened but often not in the exact way it really did happen. Doubtless Natalie's

163

view of his narrative is also distorted, but it is enough to convince us that the reality and Félix's narrative do not absolutely coincide. Félix's version, as we recall it, may seem at moments to dissolve to make room for what Madame de Mortsauf's or Natalie's would have been; and these different versions combine to wrap the events in space.

7

When we speak of "seeing" a character, there is always a certain ambiguity in the word. We mean both that we have a sense of his appearance, as he enters a room, for example, and also that we recognize him for himself and no one else. Our eyes discern a man in a grey coat, half a block away, waiting for a bus at a street corner. As we come nearer, we recognize him as a friend. The experience is different from what it was a moment ago when we merely saw the figure waiting beside the curb; it is also different from our thoughts of our friend when he is not there. We recognize Balzac's characters as people whom we have met, whom we like or dislike; we see them in terms of what we know of their pasts; and at the same time we feel that, like the man in the grey coat, they are really "there," standing at the curb, or walking to meet us. They are not glued to the paper or caught in some striking pose. Even when they are out of sight, we believe that, like our friend, they still exist in some real place—a house, a forest, or another street—and may reappear at any moment.

164

But real people exist in time as well as in space. As soon as we recognize our friend, we place him in terms of his past; we may also wonder about his future. Is he on his way to his office? It seems rather late for that. His bulging brief case might suggest that he is going to the station to catch a train. We wonder what train: he would miss the 10:37; perhaps it is the 11:16. If we see him again in a week, or a month, or a year, we may notice changes in him, and they will help make us realize how time has passed since we met him at the corner.

No novelist has been more concerned with the passing of time than Balzac, and none before *La Comédie humaine* had used such varied means to suggest it. The plunging into the midst of things and then returning to the past, for the sake of concentration and chronological perspective, has been a familiar device in poetic narration since Homer. We find occasional earlier novels that treat time very freely, such as *Tristram Shandy* and *Melmoth the Wanderer,* both of them among Balzac's favorites; but a straightforward chronological narration had been the general rule in the novel. If the novel was written in letters, they were arranged in the order of their writing. Stendhal's novels follow a rather strict chronological sequence, and after Balzac Flaubert was to return to it. We are not shown Emma's childhood until she has married Charles Bovary; but that is perhaps the most striking dislocation of time in his novels, and that is one short chapter. Of course the free use of time in the twentieth-century novel—in the works of Conrad, Proust, Faulkner and many others—is partly a result of causes outside the field of fiction; but in so far as it springs from the history of the novel itself, it owes much to Balzac.

"You meet in a salon a man whom you have not seen for ten years," Balzac writes in one of his prefaces;

he is a prime minister or a capitalist. You knew him when he didn't have an overcoat, when he showed no signs of intelligence or public spirit; you admire him in his glory; you are amazed at his fortune or his talents; then you go into a corner of the room where some charming society raconteur tells you in half an hour the picturesque story, scandalous or honorable, pretty or sordid, of the ten or twenty years you knew nothing about. Often you may not hear it until the next day, or the next month; sometimes you hear it in installments. Nothing in this world exists in a single block; everything is a mosaic. The history of the past may be told in chronological sequence, but you cannot apply the same method to the moving present.[13]

It is to give us a sense of the moving present, with the wake of the past curling and seething behind it, that Balzac treats chronology with such boldness and freedom.

Here again it is hard to choose illustrations, because almost any story could be used. I might mention first *Illusions perdues*. In form it is a huge triptych. The first part, "Les Deux Poètes," begins with a rapid sketch of many years, creating a solid sense of the provincial background and of the past that produced the two heroes of the novel, David Séchard and Lucien de Rubempré. We have the feeling of much time swiftly covered and then of one important evening that looms in our memory as it must in that of the characters,

[13] *Oeuvres complètes de Balzac* (Lévy), XXII, 522–23.

since it was to influence the rest of their lives. During the last few pages all is confusion as Lucien, caught in a swirl of events, makes up his mind to leave Angoulême.

The long middle part concerns Lucien's adventures in Paris, his rise to momentary success, and his still more rapid fall. It covers eighteen months and plunges Lucien into the world of Parisian journalism. So much is happening, his life becomes so crowded with events, that time rushes by. The third part begins as Lucien, humbled and defeated, starts home to his province; and then for half that part we are taken back to what had been happening in Angoulême during his absence. The rush of time in Paris is contrasted with its languid flow in Angoulême, emphasized by the fact that what we are being told is in retrospect, so that we feel the urge to keep pushing ahead, as we may strain forward in our seats when a car has trouble climbing a hill. At last we see Lucien once more with David; the novel ends as Lucien runs away, thinking of suicide, and encounters Vautrin.

The formal effect of the novel depends, one might say, on the contrast between Paris time and Angoulême time. When Lucien comes home, we feel that he has been away for years and yet that he has hardly been away at all. As we look back on his Paris adventures, they seem to have passed like a dream, although the part that describes them is almost as long as the other two parts together. An example of the way Balzac's manner of composing is misunderstood is the fact that in at least two English translations Parts I and III (the Angoulême parts) are printed consecutively, and

167

the middle part, the pivot of the whole structure, appears in a different volume as an independent novel.

In contrast to *Illusions perdues, Splendeurs et misères des courtisanes,* which might be considered its sequel, moves in general directly forward, at once concentrating in time and spreading in treatment, to emphasize a single dramatic climax. The first part covers a period of six years; the second part, continuing without a break, covers only a few months to May 13, 1830; the third part covers only two days, May 14 and 15; and the last part, interlocking with the third, covers also two days, May 15 and 16, with a few sentences by way of epilogue suddenly spanning years, as if to underline the concentration of the last two parts. The treatment of time could hardly be more different in these two long novels which have such close relation to each other.

If one were to make any generalization about Balzac's time schemes (and always there would be many exceptions), it would, I think, be this: he is apt to surround the central scenes of his novels and stories, which cover a relatively short period (a few weeks, or months, or perhaps a few years), with a glimpse of the past and what is, in relation to that center, the future. This prologue and epilogue do not merely illumine the central scenes but emphasize their real existence in the *present* by showing them in relation to the past from which they emerge and the future into which they dissolve, that future which they themselves will color and explain once *they* have become the past. At the beginning of *Eugénie Grandet,* for example, after Balzac has described the house in Saumur, he tells us how Monsieur

Grandet made his fortune. Such a passage is not mere "exposition," something that must be gone through before we reach the story; it is an essential part of the story. The pages that describe Grandet's rise do not drag; they move very quickly, covering years in violent foreshortening, and are balanced by the swiftness of the narrative at the end, after Grandet has died and the main drama, between himself and Eugénie, is over.

Sometimes the bathing of a dramatic present in the light cast by surrounding time has almost the effect of an altarpiece, in which we are shown a figure or group which takes up the whole central panel and on either side a series of smaller scenes—those on the left being episodes in the past life of the Divinity, those on the right, future episodes. *La Muse du département* and *Le Contrat de mariage* are arranged somewhat in this manner. In several novels, *Les Paysans,* for example, the narrative continues for many pages before returning to the past. In *Pierrette* we do not catch up with the striking opening scene until we are halfway through the story. Action or movement, as the epic poets realized, does not necessarily mean action in a straight line. It is the survival of the belief that it does, no doubt largely a matter of habit, that has made people say that there is almost no action in Proust's great and continually swirling novel.

Some critics have thought that Balzac constructs his novels as a playwright would construct a drama to be acted upon the stage. Though I think this idea is mistaken, it is easy to see how it arose. If Balzac reveals his characters largely through their talk and actions, if the central part of each book is composed of a number of scenes each one quite fully developed, what could be more simple than to tie a few such scenes together and make a play out of the novel? Of course this has often been done, sometimes with ludicrous results. Balzac himself tried to write plays, not as a rule driven by his creative urge but because he hoped to make some quick money. Gautier describes the manner, at once casual and rushed, in which he attacked these dramas, calling on his friends for help; and we have only to read them to see how little his talent was suited for the stage. Vautrin, in the play to which he gives his name, seems a caricature of the real Vautrin. He is diminished far more even than the Falstaff of *Henry IV* when he re-appears in *The Merry Wives of Windsor*. The fact that Gertrude and Pauline in the play *La Marâtre* are themselves interesting only makes us regret that Balzac did not use them in one of his novels instead of the thin and contrived medium in which they have to struggle for existence. Of all the plays, only *Le Faiseur* and *L'Ecole des ménages* give the impression that Balzac really enjoyed writing them.

The reason for this is clear. Balzac's characters take on their reality from the detail with which they are presented, from the space in which he has bathed them, and from the time through which they move—in other words, from the very form and texture of the novels that contain them. All these things must be sacrificed in a play. Most of the detail must be omitted; the space the writer had created becomes the actual space enclosed by painted scenery on the stage; the sense of time collapses, except for the short stretches coinciding with the action as performed.

170

It is interesting that three of the men who learned most from Balzac—Dostoievski, Henry James, and Proust—are psychological novelists. Balzac himself is not, if by that we mean a novelist who frequently "goes behind" to analyze the consciousness of his people. His books are full of sharply contrasted characters engaged in violent struggle; but, as Balzac says of *Les Secrets de la princesse de Cadignan,* they are dramas "not suitable for the stage." The whole evolution of Balzac's method, on the other hand, through the groping years of his youth to the triumphant moment when he conceived the idea of *La Comédie humaine* transforms it into an inspired medium by which to express, in all its flow and spread, the excitement of contemporary history.

8

La Comédie humaine is not what we would usually think of as a series of historical novels, or even as one great historical novel in many parts. As a young man, inspired by Sir Walter Scott, Balzac considered producing such a series; but before long he realized that this was not the way to achieve the result he desired. The historical novel is often a kind of pseudo-history, and that was not what interested Balzac. He knew that the methods of the historian and the novelist are very different. "The historian of manners obeys harsher laws than those that bind the historian of facts," he writes in *Les Paysans.* "He must make everything seem plausible, even the truth; whereas in the domain of history properly so called, the impossible is justified by the fact that it occurred."[14] And in his *Lettres sur la Littérature* he says somewhat the same thing: "Talent appears in the depiction of the causes that beget facts, in the mysteries of the human heart whose impulses are neglected by the historians."

Here is the first sentence in the story that begins *La Comédie humaine:* "Halfway down the rue Saint Denis, almost at the corner of the rue du Petit-Lion, there formerly stood one of those precious houses which make it easy for historians, by analogy, to reconstruct Paris as it used to be."[15] It is the shop and residence of Monsieur Guillaume, La Maison du Chat-qui-pelote. We are given a solid picture of this old house, a survival of several centuries still there during the First Empire (the period of the story's action), but now (at the time of the telling some fifteen or twenty years later) already pulled down to make room for something new. It may not be accidental that Balzac chose to begin *La Comédie humaine* with a picture of historical change. His stories are full of houses, streets, whole quarters, where the sense of the past impinges upon and blends with the present.

When Lucien de Rubempré, in 1820, is taken to the Palais Royal, Balzac describes it as it was then but is no longer: "There is good reason for giving a picture of this sordid bazaar; for it played such an important

[14] *Les Paysans,* XXIII, 181.
[15] *La Maison du Chat-qui-pelote,* I, 3. *La Maison du Chat-qui-pelote* originally appeared in 1830 as *Gloire et malheur,* long before Balzac had conceived of *La Comédie humaine.* The Conard edition in placing it first in the series is following, here as elsewhere, Balzac's own latest plan for the order and grouping of the various novels and stories in the *Comédie.*

role in Parisian life for thirty-six years that few men over forty will not enjoy this description, though the younger generation will not believe it."[16] The house of the Thuillier family also "deserves an exact description, were it only to compare the bourgeoisie as it used to be with the bourgeoisie of today." In the provinces, as we would expect, the change is slower; but we are even more aware of the past, sharpening by contrast our sense of things as they are. As we walk through the quiet rooms, we feel on our faces the breath of the Restoration, because the air of the Ancien Régime, the Revolution, and the Empire—still lurking in the corners like the smell of mildew in the straw mattings of an old house by the sea—prevents our taking it for granted.

But people change more quickly than houses. Houses may recall history; but it is, after all, men and women who make it. One of Balzac's most interesting historical studies is the group of stories (with an introductory essay) that he called *Sur Catherine de Médicis;* but this series is, of course, outside the chronological framework that binds together most of *La Comédie humaine.* Within that framework the two stories that most nearly suggest the historical novel are *Les Chouans* and *Une Ténébreuse Affaire. Les Chouans* deals with the revolt of the Breton peasants under the leadership of the royalists in 1799. *Une Ténébreuse Affaire* tells of a plot by Napoleon's secret police and describes an aristocratic family with royalist sympathies between 1803 and 1806. These novels then concern the past, but the very recent past: they would correspond

[16] *Illusions perdues,* XII, 123.

with a novel written today about the First World War.

Les Chouans is set among the sunken roads, the mists and rocks of the country around Fougères, which dominates the scene from its central cliff. Its mood is one of "ferocity intensified by the fury and cruelty of party spirit." The novel begins with a dramatic incident, a skirmish between the troops of the Republic and the Chouans, followed at once by the robbing of a coach. We are thus plunged into one immediate small corner of history. But then time broadens out; we are shown the troops as they read one of Napoleon's incisive proclamations; and suddenly, as if through a rift in the fog, we have a sense of the *general* historical situation. It is only for a moment; but after this the excitement of what happens in this limited region is sharpened by our feeling that it is a detail, closely seen, of something enormous that is also happening in many other places, one eddy of the great historical tide that is sweeping Europe. In *Une Ténébreuse Affaire* we are also given one small event, and through it the very air of the time—the suspense, the restlessness, the provisional quality of the last days of the Consulate and the early days of the Empire—as felt by a group of aristocrats in the provinces. Here the relationship to world currents is shown at the end, when Laurence de Saint-Cygne finds Napoleon near Jéna on the eve of the battle and asks him to pardon her two cousins and the forest guard Michu, wrongfully condemned to death through a plot of Fouché's secret police.

Both of these novels are based remotely upon actual episodes, but these are themselves obscure and Balzac has handled them with absolute freedom. Real people hardly appear on the scene, although the ominous pres-

174

ence of Fouché is in the background and, of course, the figure of Napoleon. On her quest, at the end of *Une Ténébreuse Affaire,* before she finds Napoleon, Laurence has a short interview with Talleyrand; and the way Balzac represents Talleyrand and Napoleon is characteristic of his treatment of historical figures. If we are shown them at all, it is briefly and casually. I am sure it is no coincidence that the main exceptions— the detailed portraits of Catherine de Médicis and her court and the sketch of Louis XI in *Maître Cornélius* —concern figures of another age. Balzac does not try to capture Napoleon for us the way Tolstoi does in *War and Peace.* The only full picture of him is in the narrative of the old soldier in *Le Médecin de campagne,* and that is not Napoleon himself: it is his legend as it has survived in the memory of his men. When Laurence meets him on the eve of Jéna, Balzac shows us one glimpse of "his Caesarine face, pale and terrible," the Emperor talks for a moment, and that is all. These rare appearances of historical personages do not then compete with the fictional characters, as they do in many novels, to produce an unconvincing and curiously mixed effect rather like that of living actors interrupting an animated cartoon. We never ask ourselves: "How did Balzac know that Napoleon or Talleyrand or Louis XVIII would have felt like that? By what right does he give us these alleged intimate views?" Of course Balzac does invent what they say, but they say so little, they appear so briefly that we no more doubt their reality than we would that of any great public figure whom we saw in a parade or in a box at the theatre.

These two novels, then, with a number of short

stories and individual scenes (the Empire ball, for example, in *La Paix de ménage,* or Napoleon's review of his troops that begins *La Femme de trente ans*) form what might be called the historical threshold of *La Comédie humaine.* But its real subject is the history of the years between 1815 and 1845, to which Balzac was directly exposed. Echoes of Napoleon are everywhere, but we feel his presence as we feel that of a great man recently dead (as we now, for example, feel Franklin Roosevelt's) in the stamp he has left upon the time that followed him and in the various memories, legends, interpretations that make him still a living force. It is, after all, as they are reflected in the social consciousness that great men impress their own and succeeding generations, and not by their private talks with their wives or mistresses or by their unspoken reveries at which we can only guess.

But the historical texture of any age is made up of innumerable private talks and individual actions; and it is this texture, at once affecting and affected by political and social trends, that Balzac, interpreting his own generation by the light of his special genius, presents in *La Comédie humaine.* When Lucien and Eugène come to Paris, it is not merely to Paris: it is to the Paris of the Restoration, of Balzac's own youthful struggles; if Dinah de la Baudraye becomes the Muse of her department, it is because of her romantic desire (the fashion of the moment) to emulate George Sand. There were at the time a number of so-called "Muses" in Paris.

But to realize the present as history, that is to say, always in transformation, one must see it in relation to what has gone before. When we are shown the past of

176

Philippe Bridau or Colonel Chabert, it is not only their individual lives that impress us : it is the whole historical past of Napoleon's campaigns as they affected two of his soldiers. There were many dignified relics like Chabert and many adventurers and crooks like Philippe. When we read of how Père Grandet amassed his fortune, we see directly from the inside how such fortunes were gathered by shrewd profiteers during the upheaval of the Revolution and the Empire. There were also capable bourgeois who made their fortunes quite honestly, like César Birotteau and Père Goriot. Even the fantastic *Treize* has a remote historical justification in the secret societies with mysterious rites that flourished as a kind of aftermath of the Revolution. The main theme of both *La Vieille Fille* and *Le Cabinet des antiques* is the contrast between two generations, two ways of life. In *Béatrix* we are plunged into the gaudy Paris of the July Monarchy after our eyes have grown accustomed to the Breton twilight, with its memories not only of the Chouans but of du Guesclin; and we feel that in a few years the young Breton noble, Calyste du Guénic, has lived through a whole historical cycle. And so one might go on taking examples from nearly every novel and story in *La Comédie humaine*.

But the complete history of any period would not be the separate listing, even if such were possible, of each one of its distinct happenings. "Nothing indicates more clearly the lack of a social outlook," Balzac writes in an early book review, "than the works of some writers, who may possess talent but whose nearsightedness sees nothing in history but a number of isolated facts."[17]

[17] Review of *Les Deux Fous* by P. L. Jacob in *Le Feuilleton des Journaux Politiques* for May 5, 1830. Reprinted in *Oeuvres complètes,* XXXVIII, 429.

One must feel their interrelationship: not only the flow of one minute, one year into the next, but the simultaneity of all that each minute, each year contains. History exists in space as well as in time, and space, like time, is continuous. Therefore, as Proust remarks in *La Prisonnière,* Balzac—looking at his novels and stories, perceiving their essential unity, because all along he had thought of them in the terms of history— conceived the idea of joining them together into one vast cycle, and thus added to his work "a stroke of the brush the last and the most sublime."

9

Although *La Comédie humaine*—with its main divisions, *Etudes de moeurs, Etudes philosophiques,* and *Etudes analytiques,* headed by Balzac's famous Preface —did not appear until 1842, the systematic use of recurring characters began as early as 1833. Of the three groups, the *Etudes analytiques,* consisting merely of the *Physiologie du mariage* and *Petites Misères de la vie conjugale,* need not concern us here. Although a number of characters from the *Etudes de moeurs* are mentioned in the latter, neither book is a novel: they are discussions of marriage as an institution illustrated by fictional anecdotes. The *Etudes philosophiques,* on the other hand, are a central part of the *Comédie.* Balzac has placed under that rubric the more obviously symbolic novels, such as *La Peau de chagrin;* those in which there is most discussion of abstract ideas, such as *Louis Lambert;* and a scattering of tales whose setting, very often, is in the past. The divisions of the *Etudes de moeurs, Scènes de la Vie de province, Scènes de la Vie parisienne,* and so on, explain themselves, except for the *Scènes de la Vie privée* which, as Balzac tells us, deal especially with youthful characters.

These divisions need not be taken too seriously. They are not even the best guide for the order in which *La Comédie humaine* should be read, since they follow no chronological or historical scheme. One could say, for example, that the *Etudes philosophiques* might better come before the *Etudes de moeurs,* because many of the stories take place at an earlier period and because in others are expressed, at once in a more general and more explicit form, some of the ideas that keep appearing less obviously throughout the *Etudes de moeurs.* Balzac himself, in *Les Comédiens sans le savoir,* refers to "the winding and capricious course of these Etudes." One feels that, if he had lived longer and written still other novels, he would have changed the order and grouping of the various parts with each new edition. He must have placed his stories here and there with something of the loving pleasure that a man may feel in rearranging the sets of stamps in his albums or the books in his library.

It would be hard to exaggerate, however, the importance of the unification. Critics have said that it reduces the impression of size, that Balzac's Paris in which we are constantly meeting the same people—the doctors Desplein and Bianchon, the bankers Nucingen and du Tillet, the journalists Blondet and Lousteau— seems more like a provincial town than a great metro-

179

polis. The plan has been blamed as hampering Balzac's creative freedom, as being arbitrary and mechanical, as destroying the effect of surprise or spontaneity. I do not think that such criticisms are valid. Of course, one can choose no manner of presentation, in any of the arts, without sacrificing certain things for the sake of certain others. The question is where does the balance lie, is the gain worth the sacrifice? In this case, I feel that Balzac has gained immeasurably more than he has lost.

As for the suggestion that Paris seems reduced and limited, we must remember that although Paris was a large city when Balzac wrote, it was scarcely more than one-quarter the size that it is today. In Balzac's Paris we are shown a dozen or more groups whose edges flow into each other. If we notice the reappearance of characters, it is because they are the ones to whom we have been introduced; but we are also constantly meeting new faces. There are many other doctors besides Bianchon and Desplein, many other lawyers besides Derville. The reader at first does not remember them so well precisely because he does not meet them so often; and looming behind these lesser figures are the anonymous crowds, at the opera, in the streets, in the rows of mysterious houses that we do not enter. If meeting a few of the same figures in *Le Père Goriot* and *Illusions perdues,* let us say, makes us realize that even in the biggest city we may run across people we know, it also makes us realize that the Paris of *Le Père Goriot,* the Paris of *Illusions perdues* and of many other stories are aspects of the *same* Paris, which includes them all and infinitely transcends each one. It is just the opposite of the feeling we have in reading a number of Parisian novels where the characters never reappear—that the special Paris of each story is separated from the rest as if by a glass partition, so that we cannot step from one to the other.

As for the objection that the scheme is hampering or mechanical, the real answer is the one that Proust suggests: namely, that it was not a scheme arranged in advance and imposed from without, but one that, like everything else that has to do with the form of Balzac's novels, evolved from the very nature of the subject. No one probably would deny that Balzac, in the enthusiasm of his revisions, may at times have forced the note. We occasionally meet characters, in different stories, who bear the same name but whose identity is only nominal. In most of these cases the characters had originally different names, and Balzac rechristened one or the other, for the sake of his unifying scheme. It would be hard to defend as a formal procedure his habit of calling attention to the relation between stories by an italicized *See Le Père Goriot* or *See Illusions perdues* within parentheses. The parentheses, however, suggest that he considered such notes not as real parts of the text but rather as practical helps to the reader.

But there would be no reason for Balzac's unifying scheme if all one could say for it was that it did *not* have a limiting effect: its virtues are of the most affirmative sort and are the direct expression of what is most personal in Balzac's genius.

This scheme might be described as doing for the whole series, on a grand scale, what Balzac had done separately in almost every part. When we think of

La Comédie humaine as a single work, such novels as
Les Chouans and *Une Ténébreuse Affaire* give us more
fully the sense of the immediate past of which we are
reminded as we read of the youth of Colonel Chabert
or Père Grandet or Père Goriot. Each novel itself becomes one of the lighted shapes, so carefully presented,
which pattern the surrounding shadow in most of the
individual books, and that shadow becomes the space
that exists between them. When the characters reappear, they do not step out of nowhere; they emerge
from the privacy of their own lives which, for an interval, we have not been allowed to see. Just as Proust
(after giving us the sense of time's moment by moment
passing as he describes the growth and withering of
Swann's love for Odette) suddenly hides Swann and
presents him an older and somewhat different person
after a lapse of time, so Balzac brings back his characters after time has passed over them, and our total
impression of any such character is not derived merely
from his first appearance. In *Le Lys dans la vallée* we
have a picture of the youth of Félix de Vandenesse, as
he writes to Natalie de Manerville; but Natalie herself
is not simply a name, embodied for an instant in her
caustic reply to Félix. We know her as she was before
she married, from *Le Contrat de mariage,* and so we
can picture her reading Félix's account and guess how
she may receive it—although her letter comes as a
partial surprise, because in the years since we have
seen her she has profited so much by her mother's hints
that now we feel she need take hints from nobody.
Félix we meet again in *Une Fille d'Eve,* and we see how
he too has matured. Still himself, he is no longer the

passionate boy he described to Natalie or yet the somewhat overwrought young man who described him; he has learned from experience and acquired a wisdom and detachment which he had not possessed.

This multifold way of seeing the characters enriches and explains not only them but the events in which they take part. When, at the end of *Les Mémoires de deux jeunes mariées,* we discover that Louise's husband Marie-Gaston (whom she had suspected of infidelity) has actually been helping his sister-in-law, the facts of the case might seem unconvincing if, from *La Grenadière,* we did not remember the very special relationship between Marie-Gaston and his brother when they were still boys. If we have read *Un Prince de la bohème,* we are not surprised that La Palférine is delighted to lure Béatrix away from Calyste, and we can understand the ironic pleasure the episode must have given him.

Such side illuminations are constantly occurring, but what counts even more than the added light cast upon the characters is the sense of their continuing existence; what counts above all is the sense of the time into which they disappear and from which they emerge. As we see Eugène de Rastignac during his successful career, we remember his early days in the Maison Vauquer and what has happened during the intervening years. When, in *Le Député d'Arcis,* we come back into the region that we knew from *Une Ténébreuse Affaire* and meet descendants of the characters we had seen in the earlier book, we are given a sudden insight into the difference between those two periods, the first days of the Empire and the July Monarchy. We feel this difference not from the outside, as shown by a diagram of political

183

events whose dates we must try to remember, but from the inside, as the people themselves felt it; and the events become part of living experience. When in *La Cousine Bette* we meet the fine old Maréchal Hulot and recognize him as the Major Hulot who had fought against the Chouans forty years ago, it is as if we had lived through two generations; we have seen the fall of Napoleon and his brief return, the years of the Restoration and the July Monarchy—and those years have been crowded with figures, figures changing with time as everything changes.

But history is not merely a vertical column of events; it is also a horizontal spread: at any moment myriads of things are occurring, each one in some manner acting upon all the others. As soon as we have penetrated a short way into *La Comédie humaine,* we feel that each book is charged not only with its own life but with the life of the whole. In the same glance we see both Paris and the provinces, and in both we see a multitude of people all *at that very moment* living. A brief reference recalls a detailed scene, and each drama becomes more intense because we place it in the midst of other dramas. It is the flow of time with its constant repetition and change, the spread of space with its recurring patterns and its variety, and yet the continuity of both, the inter-relationship of the different parts of each, that Balzac recreates for us in *La Comédie humaine;* and what is this sense of the continuity in which all life exists but the sense of History itself?

10

Perhaps now we can imagine, however dimly, something of what Balzac felt as he wrote at his table through the long hours of the night. Proust has described the creative excitement, the ecstasy that seized him as he recaptured his own past. It would seem that Balzac was able to reach that same sense of communicating with direct reality, through a kind of memory that was not limited to his immediate personal experience. Just as Proust saw the flow of his own life, Balzac saw the flow of the life of his whole generation: it was as if he could remember not only for himself but for everyone else as well. We might almost say that the vitality of his characters came not so much from his ability to see them and analyze them as from his being able to create for himself their memories, their surviving pasts. He must have been able to keep for hours at a time, derived from the innermost depths of his genius, an excitement, a tension that we may faintly approach now and then through the help of something outside ourselves—a great piece of music, perhaps, or a special light over the sea.

Speaking of Balzac's memory, Gautier writes: "That wonderful gift of his youth, Balzac kept it throughout his life, intensified even, and it is through it that his enormous labor may be explained."[18] Balzac himself, in *Ferragus,* refers to memory as "the sole quality through which we live," and Louis Lambert "not only recalled

[18] Théophile Gautier, *Portraits contemporains* (nouvelle edition; Paris, 1898), p. 58.

objects at will; but he could see them situated, lighted, colored as they were when he had first perceived them." This memory is very close to creative imagination; but, as Balzac said again and again, it would have been largely wasted without the energy, the persistence that allowed him to make full use of it. Often, no doubt, the spark was only kindled after agonizing hours when it took all his courage to keep from complete despair.

But this memory, or imagination, was helped by another important gift: "To forget is the great secret of strong creative lives," Balzac writes in *César Birotteau,* "to forget as nature forgets, nature who is not aware of what is happening, for whom each hour is the beginning of her indefatigable creation."[19] This might seem to contradict what he has written about the importance of memory, and yet actually the ideas complement each other: without forgetting there can be no effective remembering. As we look over Balzac's life with its swarm of worries and distractions, we can see that he must have been able to forget almost at will. What he forgot were the struggles of the man Balzac whom Balzac the creator could observe, as he observed, to transmute into material, everything that was a part of his age.

Louis Lambert, he tells us, remembered things just as they were at the moment when he perceived them. If this is true, then perhaps Balzac's own memory was different from that of his character. For does not the visionary quality of which Baudelaire speaks depend on the creative gift of recalling things *not* as originally observed—as discrete fragments existing at one special

[19] *César Birotteau,* XIV, 315.

186

point in time and space—but rather transformed and electrified by being surrounded by "history," by the infinite variety of everything else?

Although each novel has its own pattern, *La Comédie humaine* was never finished. Balzac listed the titles of books he meant to write, to be included in this or that part; but even if he had lived to write them all, he would still have been seeing new stories, imagining new people. As it exists, then, this great work has not the clear proportions of a sonata movement. It is more like a gigantic but uncompleted fugue, developing episode after episode with no hint of an end. Perhaps, since history itself has no end, it is appropriate that it was not finished; that, with the sense it gives us of the past forever flowing into and coloring the present, there is no line fixed between itself and the future.

BIBLIOGRAPHICAL NOTE

Bibliographical Note

This study is based primarily on a close reading and rereading of the *Oeuvres complètes de Honoré de Balzac* (texte revisé et annoté par Marcel Bouteron et Henri Longnon; Paris: Conard, 1912-40), Tomes I to XL. Occasional citations from Balzac's prefaces to early editions and from youthful works not included in the Conard edition are indicated in the footnotes.

There would be no point in listing all the books and articles about Balzac read in preparation for this study. I should like, however, to mention a few of the more recent volumes that I found most helpful and to express my gratitude to their authors.

First among such works would be *A Balzac Bibliography,* by William Hobart Royce (Chicago, 1929). I should like also to call the reader's attention to Royce's lively little book, *Balzac as He Should Be Read* (New York, 1946), which arranges the stories in a logical and chronological order (not such an easy task as it might seem) and suggests a smaller group of key works for those who have not time to tackle the whole *Comédie humaine.* Another most useful reference book is *Les Idées de Balzac d'après La Comédie humaine,* by Geoffroy Atkinson (Geneva and Lille, 1949-50), Tomes I to V. In this work Mr. Atkinson has carefully sorted and arranged under various headings Balzac's opinions and ideas (as distinct from those of his characters) and has set them in relief by pointed comments of his own.

191

My main source for biographical material was Balzac's correspondence. References to the various collections from which I have quoted may be found in the footnotes. Among biographical works, I should mention *La Jeunesse de Balzac,* by Gabriel Hanotaux and Georges Vicaire (Paris, 1921), and the three volumes by L.-J. Arrigon, *Les Débuts littéraires d'Honoré de Balzac* (Paris, 1924), *Les Années romantiques de Balzac* (Paris, 1927), and *Balzac et la Contessa* (Paris, n.d.). *Balzac, Homme d'Affaires,* by René Bouvier (Paris, 1930), and *Les Comptes dramatiques de Balzac,* by René Bouvier and Edouard Maynial (Paris, 1938), are also very interesting and by no means limited to an account of Balzac's finances. These were among the twentieth-century works used to check the writings of Balzac's contemporaries—Laure Surville, Gautier, Gozlan, Werdet, and others. The biographies by Stefan Zweig and André Billy each present a vivid full-length picture of Balzac, but their scope does not allow them the thorough treatment of the more specialized volumes. A. Prioult's *Balzac avant La Comédie humaine* (Paris, 1936), with its exhaustive bibliography, is indispensable for his early reading, and Fernand Baldensperger's *Orientations etrangères dans l'Oeuvre de Balzac* (Paris, 1927), for his acquaintance with foreign literatures.

Two of the books that discuss most clearly and fully Balzac's attitudes and ideas are Philippe Bertault's *Balzac et la Religion* (Paris, 1942) and Bernard Guyon's *La Pensée politique et sociale de Balzac* (Paris, 1947). A curious Marxist interpretation is given in V. Grib's *Balzac, A Marxist Analysis* (trans-

lated from the Russian by Samuel G. Bloomfield; New York, 1937).

There are so many admirable books about Balzac's genius that it is hard to choose which to include, even if one limits one's choice to fairly recent publications. I feel indebted to E. Preston's *Recherches sur la Technique de Balzac* (Paris, 1926) and Maurice Bardèche's *Balzac Romancier* (Paris, 1940) for their precise analysis of various aspects of his craftsmanship. Among books dealing more generally with his nature and his aesthetic, I shall mention only *Créatures chez Balzac,* by Pierre Abraham (Paris, 1931), *Balzac,* by Ernst-Robert Curtius (translated by Henri Jourdan; Paris, 1933), *Balzac,* by Ramon Fernandez (Paris, 1943), and *L'Esthétique du Roman Balzacien,* by H. U. Forest (Paris, 1950). There are two little books, quite different from each other, which I found perhaps the most revealing of all: *Avec Balzac,* by Alain (Paris, 1937), and *Balzac Visionnaire,* by Albert Béguin (Geneva, 1946).

Throughout my book the opinions expressed are based upon my contact with Balzac through his various writings. That these opinions have been influenced and clarified by the comments of others is certain, though it is often hard to draw the line between attitudes independently arrived at and those that have been colored by suggestion from outside. Just as sometimes an image may enter one's mind without one's being sure whether it is the recollection of an actual experience or a moment recaptured from a dream, so may one mistake the echo of something read long ago for an original idea.

INDEX

Index

Titles of the writings by Balzac referred to in the text are listed alphabetically under the heading: Balzac, Honoré de, works of. Writings by other authors are placed under the author's name or (if the name is nowhere mentioned) in the general alphabetical list.

Names of characters in Balzac's works are listed in the general index, followed by the titles of the novels in which they appear. Many characters appear in several different novels. In such cases I have mentioned only the novels or stories in which they figure most prominently or which seem most relevant to my discussion. Names of characters in the works of novelists other than Balzac are listed only if not identified by the context.

198

199

203